Authorpreneurship

HAZEL EDWARDS

Authorpreneurship

Second Edition

Acknowledgement

Thanks to my digital mentor, Kim Edwards.

'All ideas begin with encouragement, and the creative climate which accepts the necessary risk of failure from experiment and innovation.'

Published in 2024 by Amba Press, Melbourne, Australia.
www.ambapress.com.au

This book was first published in 2012 by Keesing Press.

Cover design: Tess McCabe
Proofreader: Sarah Fallon
Cartoonist: Sheila Hollingworth

ISBN: 9781922607942 (pbk)
ISBN: 9781922607959 (ebk)

A catalogue record for this book is available from the National Library of Australia.

Contents

Contents

1: What is Authorpreneurship?

Authorpreneurship

Author = originator

Entrepreneur = seller who initiates

The business of creativity is changing, not just in the formats in which ideas are presented internationally but also how authors perceive themselves.

Today, a creator needs to be an 'authorpreneur'. Apart from crafting words or images for specific audiences, this means learning the marketing, publicity, technological, legal and entrepreneurial skills to establish and maintain creative self-employment in the business of ideas.

'Author' includes any self-employed creators in the core business of ideas, whether illustrator, designer, writer or multi-skilled innovator in various mediums. Many are very small businesses or sole traders in ideas but unless they operate in a business-like manner, they will not survive.

IP (Intellectual Property) is the core business while time, energy and idea management is part of the process. Great ideas will not reach audiences unless the creators can stay in business and survive financially.

Even those who find the concept of linking creativity and business a philosophical challenge will find common sense approaches here. Beginners, mid-career and established creators alike will find strategies to use tomorrow in *Authorpreneurship*. Constant innovation and the need to keep up can be overwhelming, especially when you are the only person to do it all.

This book is about sharing strategies which enable you to work effectively at what you most enjoy doing, but also provide ways for you to streamline the process, so you can sell your ideas for longer, in varied new formats and to larger audiences. 'Authorpreneurship' is about investing in your creativity, without becoming exhausted or overwhelmed.

The concept of 'authorpreneurship' is a constant but the authors who practise 'authorpreneurship' need to be flexible in adapting to change and learning new skills and even new terms for processes that have not yet become mainstream.

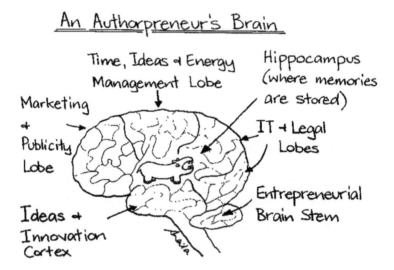

Hazel Edwards OAM (www.hazeledwards.com) has published over 200 books for adults and children, with mainstream and small publishers. Best known for *There's a Hippopotamus on Our Roof Eating Cake*, which has been constantly in print and adapted across other media for over 44 years, Hazel also runs book-linked workshops on 'Authorpreneurship' and 'Writing a Non-Boring Family History'.

A recipient of the 2009 ASA Medal, Hazel was awarded the Monash University Distinguished Alumni; Education, in 2022. Widowed with two adult children and grandchildren for whom she writes a story each birthday. Recently she updated her business card from writer to 'Authorpreneur'.

> *'Open with anticipation and close with satisfaction and profit.'*
> *Your book.*

2: Profile and Professional Areas

The Author as Brand

In the Beginning

When you start writing, you don't have a name as an author. Nor do you have a profile. You just have an idea for a manuscript. So the first stage is to write that idea as well as possible for a specific audience, not just for you. If it's only for you, it's therapy. If you want more readers, you're in the business of creativity.

Profile

An author's 'profile' means that enough people know who that writer is and what kind of work is associated with that author, and are willing to follow or buy those ideas, in whatever format they appear.

This 'profile' may be linked to a website, speaking commitments, media slots and types of writing, but more importantly, it requires recognition by groups who like that kind of work.

So an author 'profile' matters. Basically, you need to ask yourself, does anyone know your name? And if so, what for? And are they willing to pay to have access to your ideas or stories? If not, what can you do about it?

Brand

It's a big shift for authors to see themselves as a 'brand'. This is where a name is being traded or linked to marketable ideas, in varied formats and income is earned.

For some, the book will not be the main income channel, but other paid work will be offered because of the existence of the book.

In the past, an author was associated with a single 'named' publisher and their distribution channel but that is now rare. A book may have several 'lives' in different formats and with different publishers and be distributed in a variety of ways. Each project may be contracted differently. The link is the author's name or brand, not the publisher. And it may be the author brand, which is more attractive than the single book.

Authorpreneurship is not just about self-promoting or self-publishing or even vanity. Author brand is part of the business of creativity. If readers like a work by a particular author, they will look for more by that name, not necessarily through a publisher. Considering the speed of publisher mergers, takeovers and fast remaindering of books, authors who consolidate their backlist titles under their brand name and make it available on their website, are more likely to make a living. Otherwise their books may have a short life of a month or so.

Author websites are as accessible as publishers' sites for international online sales. In the past, only the publisher controlled distribution of books and mainly via bookshops and book clubs. That has changed.

Although many authors consider writing a book as the hard part of the publishing process, long-term the real challenge is in marketing and distribution.

Ego or Business?

If this is your first creation, you probably don't have a recognisable 'brand' yet. For modest creators, there's also the philosophical dilemma between 'ego' and marketing. Should you be talking about yourself? You may fear this is just being egotistical.

However, talking about the public 'author brand' and the 'book' or the ideas in that work is one remove from the private person behind it. And although your 'persona' needs to be genuine, choose how much of your research, writing habits or family you are prepared to reveal. Of course this is a bit more difficult if you're writing an autobiography!

The slower 'old style' proposal to a print publisher was essentially a plea for the publisher to invest money to develop the book, market and distribute it and return 10% of the profits to the original author. The writer only wrote the book. Now the writer has become the 'authorpreneur': initiating, writing, publishing and distributing.

Although there are new channels for ideas with digital opportunities for distribution, this also means more risk and more work for an author, who must learn a suite of eSkills. Publication can be faster, but maintenance of long-term marketing of the title may be time consuming.

Both brand and income are directly linked to who holds the rights for the intellectual property of that work in those formats.

Of course the work needs to be of quality and timely – and the production needs to be of a high standard and well edited.

Authorpreneurial Hint

List five actions to establish your brand as an author. Do them asap (as soon as possible).

- Establish or update your website 'image'
- Revamp your business card with your occupation as an author
- Offer a workshop that uses the title of your book
- Acquire a regular media slot
- Develop niche expertise.

Strategic Decisions

Strategy

A 'strategy' is a plan to move you in the direction of your long-term goal, for example:

- To become self-employed as a creator
- To build a digital business
- To research in exotic settings
- To get a book published.

A strategic thinker is likely to initiate rather than just react to others' demands. Or at least choose those demands to which s/he will react. Two people may appear to be doing the same activity, but their motives may differ, and only one may be acting strategically.

Why be strategic? Because it saves time and saves you from becoming frustrated. Because you've planned what your reactions will be to certain types of offers, anticipatory anxiety is removed. You need to know why you are doing it.

- Is it just a pleasant distraction?
- Are you unable to say 'No'?
- Is it strategic for you?

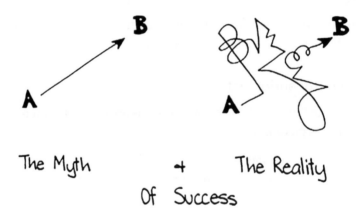

The Myth + The Reality
Of Success

Quantity

Is there any connection between effort and result? In the long-term, yes but not always immediately. Working hard or for long periods and working strategically are not always the same.

Often novice writers mistakenly judge progress only by the number of words written. Obviously it's necessary to produce, but format, subject and timing may also be strategic. And can you provide evidence of an audience? (Not just your mum!)

- How many hours did you spend writing that piece? (If you don't know, what does this indicate?)
- How many words did you write? Were they rough or polished?
- If no one buys or reads it, has your work been wasted?

- Did you check on the potential readership before starting?
- Would 'tweaking' it for a specific audience help get a contract or broader sales? For example, adding curriculum links for educators or notes for discussion groups?
- Networking with colleagues to become aware of shared challenges, possible markets and specific requirements. Occasionally the 'cappuccino approach' of having a strategic coffee may be more effective than isolation.
- Inspirational genius is unreliable. Consider the strategy of slow accumulation (i.e. consistent work). Spend an hour daily doing some of the minutiae, which lead to your eventual goal, otherwise the volume is overwhelming.
- If you 'do' enough times, with the aim of accumulating skills, polished work or contacts, that's different from the gamble of haphazard procrastinating.
- Do you initiate appointments or projects of the kind you desire, accepting that not all of them will eventuate? One in ten might be a reasonable return on 'punts'. But if you plan to try an extra punt every week, then by the tenth week, the odds are in your favour.
- A regular 'punt' or 'extra' in the direction of the kind of work you wish to do, can be strategic. An example would be to follow up leads on the last day of every month.

Quality

Then there's the issue of quality. One best seller may be the result of either many discarded, hidden projects or 'cannibalised' ones which re-use knowledge or extracts from prior, unpublished work.

Often it's hard to analyse where you should put your time and energy. Seduced by the stimulation of the next project, you start that, rather than assess what worked or didn't work in the previous period, and apply this knowledge to improve future quality.

Fatigue can affect judgement. Is the work of the highest quality or have you worn yourself out? Make judgements when you are rested, and make important decisions when fresh.

Don't send off work without checking it and make sure you have some sleep first. It's easy to press 'send' but preferable to wait until the morning to check with a clear brain. Check whether all the links are in place and whether they are logical or not. Sending hasty, unchecked material may ruin your single chance to be read, although occasionally it's better to send an 85% quality by deadline, than nothing.

Evaluation

- Keep a backwards diary (list) of what you did achieve.
- Divide into achievements and flops.
- Colour code your 'useless' list in green, 'try again' in yellow or 'done' in red.
- Against the 'try again' note the imaginative detour you'll try next.
- Have a ratio between 'original' work, recycling and administration and don't spend all your time keeping lists.
- Colour code strategic decisions, so you can find them, and re- apply.
- What can now be re-used as a generic strategy/practice?

Strategies, which have worked for others:

- Centring interviews and meetings in a home/own-office. This saves travel and examples are easily available. If meeting with collaborators use alternate venues.
- Paying for one on one tuition on a skill you need rather than enrolling for a course or teaching yourself slowly by trial and error.
- Offering consultancies via video call in lieu of personal visits to remote regions.
- Learning one eSkill per day.
- Using guest blogs on high profile sites for interviews about the writing process using recent eBook examples and tagged to your own website. These can be re-used by linking websites, which also helps the host sites.
- Uploading photos and links to Facebook as a way of accumulating anecdotes for a quarterly newsletter.
- Archiving newsletters on your website especially for re-use of feature articles in newsletter.
- Choosing a 'how to write' subject with broad appeal for an eBook.
- Having a map to check locations before saying 'yes'.
- Saying 'No' without guilt.

Saying No

- Prepare. Be aware of those situations where you've been caught before.
- Listen to the request. Agree with the praise 'Yes, you are good at ....' Wait.
- Say 'No' at least twice.
- When the emotional blackmail comes, 'But if you don't do it ....'
- Say 'No' again politely. Your tone is vital.
- Offer an alternative. A colleague may wish to do that kind of work. But don't dob in an unwilling mate!
- Offer an alternative skill, at another time, or with conditions.

Hints for assessing whether to say a 'strategic' no:

- Does it fit with your long-term goals?
- What is the ratio of preparation and anxiety versus outcome?
- What about the enjoyment factor? Could you do with a change of scene or role?
- Are you flattered to be asked?
- Has it been a quiet period and you're feeling vulnerable?
- What is the calibre of others involved?
- Why have they asked you? Have others refused? If so, why?
- What is the fee?
- What is your gut reaction?

Is Being an Early Uptake Innovator Strategic or Not?

Much depends upon timing and whether you are an early innovator, your work has novelty value and your book can become the case study example. Ask yourself, 'is everyone else doing that?'

Book trailers, blogs or apps for picture books are examples where early innovators had their books publicised via the process of educating others.

Investing in new equipment can be costly in areas where technology is outdated fast. Of course, your material will also be outdated quickly if it is tied to that technological version. Being a second or third version user may be more strategic.

So you need to personally evaluate the time invested for the financial and skills return. It may be more strategic to be part of the second uptake or a variation on what others are doing. Ask yourself what works best for your needs and the time available.

'Is Blogging a Waste of Time?' was written in 2009 as a current affair. Now it's ancient history.

Many unskilled writers have flooded the Internet and each blogger is seeking quality content from other contributors to maintain their output. So guest blogs are no longer as strategic, but their historic case study is relevant.

Is blogging and podcasting a waste of time?

I've been asked this question three times in the last week but there is no definitive answer. Individuals have to make up their own minds.

Overnight, blogs and podcasts initiate discussion, interviews or even reviews. But if you already have an author/illustrator website as your shop-front window for publicising and selling your books and talks, the question you need to ask would be, is blogging and podcasting a waste of time for a writer? Or are you altruistically acting as a hub for others?

- Technically and financially, blogs and podcasts are becoming more accessible. But if you spend your 'writing' time blogging, or podcasting are you wasting hours which could be better spent on your major literary project?
- Is your blog or podcast a 'warm-up' for other work?
- Does it raise your profile as a writer?
- Is it more than egotistical ramblings?
- Is your blog or podcast just about you, a significant challenge or about events involving others?
- If people link to your blog or podcast, does it sell more of your books? Or do you just have more links that may not be used much, a bit like thousands of unknown Facebook friends?
- For a professional, blogging or podcasting is part of the free sharing of ideas. Is that what you wish to do or does a monthly web update fulfil the same role of informing readers?
- Does learning how to blog or podcast increase your electronic skills? Is this worthwhile in itself?
- Will others pay for your later published work, if you provide early freebies? Or will you provoke more interest in future paid publications?

- How often should entries or podcasts be made?
- Does it matter at which stage of your career you are blogging or podcasting? Are you just beginning, in mid-career, blooming or defunct?
- Is a blog or podcast a substitute diary? How personal is too much? Or is the aim info-tainment? Do you have paid advertisements on it?
- Does your blog or podcast include any humour or wit, information or fascinating style?

I've decided against having a blog or podcast, but others argue that they work well for them. Decide what works best for you. And decide on content by examining those blogs and podcasts you visit often and why.

Writing this was a way of clarifying the issue and my subsequent strategy is to contribute guest blogs and podcasts of high profile bloggers and podcasters with broad readership and listener links. It's essential to also ensure you supply the tag information with the International Standard Book Number (ISBN) linked back to a book for sale on your website. Now I contribute to guest blogs and podcasts as part of a publicity campaign for my current titles, picking up on issues relevant to others and using one of my books as the example.

Workshop-Contributed Warnings of Non-Strategic Bad Habits

Other bad habits that can waste time without supporting your strategic goals are:

- Too much back-up duplication due to fear of losing files
- Too many 'lists'
- Frustration with multiple, meaningless passwords and terminology
- Too many earlier files in outmoded formats
- Learning the process takes more time than producing the original
- Miscalculating: Will an hour spent now, save you days later? Maybe not.

Authorpreneurial Hint

List two strategic changes in your work style. Do them across the next two weeks.

Asking for Payment and Costing Your Time

Looking back over the past year, what has been your most satisfying project? And how will you balance 'love' jobs and paid work in the coming year? Does passion need to be considered as a variable also? These are questions I've been asked and have thought about. Think about what your answers to them might be.

Costing: Guess-timates

Many drafts of a book may take up to a year and that's extremely difficult to budget. How can you 'cost' that time spent? There's emotional cost and financial cost as well as the time involved.

So you're really costing the experiences or the work style of being a creator. But what are you going to charge and to whom will the invoice be sent?

- A publisher?
- Your family?
- Friends?
- Yourself?

Do you need a business plan, a financial advisor or a therapist?

'I have to keep re-writing until it's finished,' admits one novelist. 'When I start, I can't say exactly how many minutes, months or years it will take.'

Costing fiction is more difficult than costing non-fiction. Some never make a living from their writing. Others want to have some control over the effort/return ratio. Former journalists who write long non-fiction books are often more realistic about the time involved in producing a book and keep to a deadline, word count and hourly estimate or even a guess-timate.

Those with extended or young families and home offices, do as much as they can, or sleep less, but this can't be maintained indefinitely. Health costs need to be considered too.

There is also the variable of whether you are writing on 'spec' (speculation), to an expression of interest with a deadline or to a contract with a brief. Do you need to 'quote' or is there a set fee? Or if juggling the time is entirely up to you admit to yourself that it's a 'love job'.

Guess-timates

Costing 'original' writing is different from costing hourly speaking or the associated paid work which comes from having written a print or eBook. Apart from advances, twice yearly royalties, or rare film options, the book may stimulate reviews, subsidiary rights such as magazine extracts, apps or paid invitations to speak.

These bookings may relate to writing techniques or to the subject of your research. For example, one non-fiction writer now escorts cruise ship specialist tours in their subject.

If you're the only one doing your specialty, decide the hourly minimum you will accept and then do your sums. You need to have an estimate of how long it will take to research and write the project. Regardless of your answer, add 10% longer and 10% for extra costs. This is a contingency fee.

Deciding what to charge is a challenge. If you go too high you will be unlikely to receive further invitations. On the other hand if you charge too little or offer to work for free you may then be taken for granted. There are rates available from professional organisations and being able to quote these makes it easier for the shy creator to be assertive and confident in seeking payment when asked to speak about their work style or project. They can say:

> *'I charge Australian Society of Authors rates which are available on their website.'*

However, the market rate may differ from the suggested professional rate and this is where networking is vital. Find out what others are charging for comparable work and recognise that payment also depends on where you are in your career. For beginning authors, there is little demand paid or unpaid, and you may be writing 'on spec'. For high profile, well published authors, there is reasonable demand and payment.

The most challenging area to cost is when you are 'in between', as a mid-list author or when you may be attempting innovative work in an area for which you have neither reputation nor backlist. If you are 'learning on the job' then it is most likely that you will pay for your own apprenticeship.

What should you do if you're offered a fee that is lower than your normal rate? What if you're offered flowers, a pen or nothing? What if you're asked to donate copies of your book for their charity and, even more vexing, you actually approve of that charity?

Many 'nice' groups assume creators will be eager to talk about their work for free; that selling copies afterwards will be sufficient recompense. Wrong!

Unless they have negotiated a higher discount from their publisher for occasions when selling their own titles, or they are self-published, if the author sells $200 worth of books after that one hour event, at 10% of the recommended retail price they will have earned a total of $20. This is minus travel and working time when they could have been producing more books. Although some people assume a writer should work for the self-satisfaction of the project from which others may benefit, this may be a by-product, but should not be the only return.

Avoid Serial Pestering

A one-book writer asks:

> What things are acceptable for me to give myself a name or generally promote, and what actions look more like overreaching myself, and coming across as if big-noting? For example, receiving positive, initial responses when approaching blogs, festivals (including emerging writer festivals), bookshops etc but then receiving no further responses, even to follow up attempts. Don't want to risk looking like a serial pest. Am I attempting to be too much of an author entrepreneur too soon? How do I know the fine line between what is acceptable and inadvertently looking cocky?

Three tries is fair enough: one try and two follow-ups. After that, you may be pestering. But if money is owed, that's a different matter.

Hints for the Money Balancing Act

- Plan different rates for corporate, community, not for profits or 'freebie' private charities. Decide these at the beginning of a year, and list them either near or on your phone/computer for easy reference.
- Clarify whether these are for one-off use, or include repeats. For example, if your author talk or written work is recorded in any medium for later usage, even on another campus, or put on YouTube, the fee may be higher. Quality control is another issue here. Amateur clips circulating which contain extracts from your ideas out of context are an embarrassment.
- The quandary for an author-speaker is that you need the audience to buy your book, rather than take a free recording of your talk or written extract for other use.

- Clarify the length of your speaking commitment. Often travel and setting-up time may turn an hour into a half day, or recovery from fatigue may mean a non-productive next day.
- Spread research costs over several projects. Multiple use of research may mean writing fiction as well as non-fiction, or for the trade as well as the schools market.
- Community groups or corporate groups often want an organisational history or 'how to' written, but are unrealistic about the time and costs involved. When they learn that a professional would ask the equivalent of a senior university academic's salary for a year, plus the actual costs of production, many drop the project. Others apply for a grant.
- Groups who are writing grant applications often ask for a letter of support or a detailed proposal from a prospective writer. Are you willing to spend this time freely or do you have a generic quote on file?
- Avoiding debts (where they owe you):
  - Issue an invoice beforehand so you can be paid on the day. Alternatively, arrange for a half payment on signing of the contract and half on completion, rather than on publication which can often be delayed or postponed.
  - Have a standard electronic invoice template complete with ISBN, GST, ABN and contact details which can be issued quickly.
  - Some organisations prefer to pay before the end of a financial year. Make use of that knowledge. It is also handy to know that some councils will even pay in advance.

Getting the Love Job versus Paid Work Balance

- Include a 'soul project' which you do for passionate interest in a particular subject. Serendipitous job offers result from a 'passion' and because you do writing you are passionate about so well, others also become attracted to non-conventional projects.
- For most freelancers/self-employed, January is a quiet, no income month. Use quiet months to prepare generic publicity such as photos, bios and business proposals, write a big project or research in a remote location. Upgrade your equipment and learn to use it in this period.
- Think outside the 9am-5pm routine. There's no need to panic over no money coming in that month if you are aware of other possibilities at peak times later in the year.

- Think in blocks of time. May and October are peak literary festival times. Plan author-talk travel, but prepare content in January. Co-ordinate speaking commitments geographically. Do two to three events in the same direction.
- Consider publicity as work. Pace yourself to avoid fatigue and a bad temper.
- Average your income across the whole year, even if the 'front' payments occur only three or four times.
- Balance some short, quick paying, small events or mini writing projects with longer ones. Have a series so that characters or settings are already established and artwork can be re-used.
- Aim for two to three days per week of bread and butter regular income. Anything extra can be considered hundreds and thousands ... or millions.
- Costs must be set against income. Costs may include:
  - Home office including electronic updates
  - Travel/accommodation/car maintenance
  - Professional subscriptions/postage/couriers
  - Agency fees
  - Insurance

Doing Freebies

Charitable acts should be private. In other words, you decide you will not charge rather than have the host assume you will do a 'freebie'.

These may include schools attended by your family, favourite charities or personal favours.

- Decide what kind of work you are prepared to do without charging. For example, some authors agree to a Fundraiser Dinner Talk where their time is the donation and the host can publicise the event and charge in aid of their favourite charity.
- Be wary of planning extra paid work around a vague charitable event in a remote location on a difficult date which is then cancelled (e.g. New Year's Day). Get confirmation in a businesslike way, even if negotiating with a charity.
- If 'free' books for celebrity auctions or organisational 'events' are the charitable request, check on arrangements for postage (especially if international), collection or even acknowledgement they have been

received by the charity. If it is a generic request with the wrong name, ignore it. Some groups write to every author online.

- Is this 'learning on the job' in a new area where you need to gain skills?
- Is it collaborative where you will be learning with a colleague or returning a favour?
- Is this likely to lead to other paid or satisfying work?
- What's your ratio of paid versus love jobs: 1/10, 50/50%, 100%? Which way?

Variables:

- Size of audience?
- How far away is it/what is the travelling time?
- Is it likely to lead to recommendations for more, similar work?
- Philosophically, you are in tune?
- They are genuine fans of your work.
- You need to sell some of your pile of books.

Money Strategies

Your strategy needs to reflect your goals and the career stage you have reached.

How much do you intend to invest in your writing career and for how long? Expect a loss for the first two to three years, then re-invest a proportion into the business as you would with any start-up business. This may include a website.

A beginning author needs another part time, casual or full time job, preferably related to writerly skills. Or a wealthy, supportive partner, which is an unlikely option.

- School teaching prepares an author for public speaking which is part of an author's life today. It connects the writer to curricula so that a secondary market of future books can be accessed and establishes teacher and librarian networks.
- Lecturing can help develop your own skills e.g. running creative writing workshops.
- Journalism is craft training and establishes networks.
- Working in publishing helps with industry knowledge.

Others prefer an intensively physical job to contrast with the mental aspect of writing.

Diversify

Look at writing across genres and areas – e.g. educational books bring in income, PLR (Public Lending Right) and ELR (Educational Lending Right). Fiction is the 'glamour' area but can be the least reliable area of income.

Distinguish between the 'publicity' of talking about your recent book (which may be a 'freebie' in the week the book is released) and running a creative writing workshop. Workshops must be paid at ASA rates as this sells your 'how to write' skills rather than your books.

Network to find the 'going' rate and conditions.

- Publicise your skills for the type of work you desire.
- 'Follow up' on earlier colleagues and offer an idea taster of your new skills.
- Decide on the general direction of your goal, even if detours occur.
- Think outside 9am-5pm and weekdays.
- Don't see 'networking' as always about you. Help others too.
- Recommend another who is more appropriate for a particular job at the time.
- Answer this question: what type of work will you never do again?
  - Vague requests, no fee offered and the person is indecisive.
  - They get your name wrong.
  - A committee must approve the content. And they rarely meet.
  - Details are missing about where, when, how many and why?
  - Their emails bounce or they don't respond quickly.
  - Directions are wrong or the brief changes at each meeting.
  - Contact person changes and they don't tell you.
  - Massive research or preparation is required but there is no contract or 'kill' fee (1/3 final fee and permission to re-use).
  - No advance but much work is required and there is no guarantee of publication.
  - They lose the paperwork or even the electronic detail you supplied.

What type of work do you seek?

- Creatively and intellectually satisfying
- Courteous and reliable colleagues

- Innovative
- Well paid
- Adds to your skills CV
- Leads to additional work in comparable fields
- Fun
- Pays on time
- High quality
- Local with no peak hour travel
- Exotic locations.

Much effective writing is a matter of time and energy management: yours.

> ## Authorpreneurial Hint
>
> List three payment initiatives/changes you will make in your work style this month. Do them. For example, require a call a week before the event confirming details about talks and payment on the day.

So You Want to Get Published?

Checklist for Potential Authors

Many first time writers, unsure of what to do with their book ideas, waste time and money on inappropriate or unnecessary work. This checklist offers ways to save time and suggests strategies.

What is your potential market? Who might want to read and/or buy your book? Is your version of the subject big enough? Test the market with articles or an extract before you attempt a book.

Non-fiction books, especially 'how tos' are easier to place than fiction. Compile the ten most common frequently asked questions (FAQs) and use answers to these as the basis of your chapters. Write a workshop manual first, trial it and collect anecdotes or case studies to broaden the appeal of your material to male/female, rural/urban, or international readership. Narrow examples will limit your sales.

Buy and analyse current books in this area. You can then decide in what ways yours could be better or different. Ask yourself whether it fits a genre and whether it is like, or differs from, a well known title.

Often a first time writer has lived through a significant medical, psychological or adventurous experience and wants to share this. Examples include divorce, grief, extreme travel or surviving cancer. This may be therapeutic writing and emotionally cathartic for the writer. However, to appeal to commercial readers it needs to have specific content, with potential value for the reader in terms of advice or vicarious experience. The initial format may be a diary, but it will need crafting.

Even if your concept sounds possible and quite imaginative, it is the initial marketing via book proposal, synopsis and sample chapters, which is more important.

Realistically it will take at least a year to research, write, workshop and market a book. Consider joining a year-long course, which offers weekly workshopping. This will provide feedback and also the discipline to keep you writing regularly (e.g. the non-fiction projects course at TAFE, writers' centres or online).

How topical is your content? Does it relate to an anniversary or a celebration such as the Olympic Games? Unless it is an eBook, you need to be writing two years in advance!

Do you have a print book? Consider other formats such as eBooks, audio, graphics or even a new format such as tweets and responses with cartoons etc.

Commercial or Self-Publishing

Are you considering commercial, co- or self-publishing? Some 'packagers' will prepare your manuscript for publication for a fee, but there's no distribution, reviewing nor publicity. Co-publishing requires you to pay part costs with some distribution links whereas commercial publishers bear all the costs as their contribution and deal with distribution for you. To do this they have to be convinced your project is commercially viable so if you are in a niche market and familiar with that audience, it may be viable to co- or self-publish, especially if you are known as an expert.

Check out links on the Australian Society of Authors website (www.asauthors.org) which offers contract advice to members, mentorships, free advice for beginners on self-publishing, and a Style File showcase space for illustrators.

Check writing centre programs for relevant workshops such as 'life writing' or specialist interest writing groups such as speculative fiction, crime, cooking or corporate writing.

Frequently author websites include a blog or an article explaining the process of writing their books.

Several writers might start from the same experience, but one manuscript will be marketable and the others will not. The following list supplies suggestions on what makes the difference:

- Personable style which is not egotistical
- Well structured content
- Apt title
- Strong conflict
- Unexpected angle e.g. the benefits of having a serious illness
- Humour
- Insight, not just 'and this happened next'
- Period or place with unique appeal
- Length
- Crafted to the specific readership or need to know
- Support from a relevant organisation that, for example, writes a foreword or will take copies for sale to members
- Contacts who will buy it
- Media worthy author.

Building Author Reputation

Reputation. Are you already known for commenting on this subject? Do you have a clippings file? Are you a columnist or do you have a regular TV or radio slot (even for a different subject)? Are you famous or notorious (these are not the same)?

Publicity. Are you willing and do you have the skill and energy to promote this book after publication?

Are you already known for giving talks on this subject? Have these talks been 'freebies' or paid invitations?

Do people contact you for advice on this topic? Does the subject have only local appeal or is it international and timeless?

Choosing Content

Content. In one sentence, what is your book about? Include the title, conflict and theme in this one sentence, for example, *Antarctic Writer on Ice* is the eDiary of a fifty-something, female, non-scientist who hates the cold and lacks the adventure gene, but who survives an Antarctic expedition, beset on a polar ship with 34 blokes, three women and a chopper crash.

Test your material with a naïve reader who knows nothing of the subject, and an expert who does. Then it's time to re-write.

Authorpreneurial Hint

List three initiatives towards getting published and add a deadline for each. For instance, you could research three appropriate publishers and analyse their submission requirements, by Sunday night.

Using Author PR Photos

Visuals are crucial for author or book promotion, since today's audience tends to be instant-visual rather than verbal.

Carry and use a mobile, digital camera or more recent device. Download and label systematically or you'll get swamped.

Keep several different resolution versions of each photo. Use high resolution for possible magazines but crop and compress for a website or to email without annoying recipients by excessive download time or filling their mailbox. Be careful – it is all too easy to accidently send the wrong size.

In downtime (such as in January), re-organise existing photos into files with a label showing a current year's author PR photo for fast use. The label might include the date such as 2024, your name, Current Author Photo (Hi res) or (Low res) or a tag which can be used by your host. Categories might include:

- Book covers
- With colleagues

- Research settings
- Quirky
- Current PR.

Apart from views of author activities, you need a head and shoulder shot of yourself for publicity. Choose a colourful head shot which looks professional or in keeping with your author image. A wildlife writer, for example, could be holding a snake.

Upload the photo onto your website. Some people prefer to use Facebook or other social media as a way of learning how to upload, but these photos can then be public.

Clarify copyright and always attribute to the photographer, if not you.

Legally, you need permission to use any children's images if they are in a photograph with you. Tip: Use appropriately aged children from your own family.

Often as a visiting author you are photographed at events by others, so ask for permission to use these later. If it is a professional shot, you may need to pay.

If you are a one book author, it's acceptable to be holding that book in the shot. However, if you have other roles it is safer to have a generic, bookless shot of just the author. Alternatively you could use different ones with each book title.

Provide a downloadable high resolution author photo on your website for media or conference organisers. This will save your time and theirs.

Keep your official photo within a year of your face-age. Airbrushing can be counter-productive especially if they have to find you at an event by matching to the photo clue.

Tag group photos at conferences as part of your news with a link to their site which indirectly promotes your host organisations.

Labelling: if you end up with too many photos with similar names, be ruthless and delete some.

Roles: Distinguish between your 'corporate/business' and approachable, quirky author shots.

Business card photo. If you have translated business cards they can benefit from a photo. This way you will be remembered after a business visit, especially in Asia.

Bookmarks, bookplates and headed notes can use a photo for memorable ID. A physical bookmark with author photo, website, book cover and ISBN details on the reverse and room for an autograph can market the author too.

Have your book covers in groups of titles, so they are streamlined into one file. Don't have background clutter in the photograph.

Vary your photos by changing jackets or use different scarves.

Shoot author and book at book promotion events for generic use later. Remember to use a book related prop.

A two-sided, laminated poster as a give-away for librarians is useful. It should include author and bio on one side, with covers and blurb on the reverse and should be updated annually.

Authorpreneurial Hint

List three ways of better using PR author visuals in your work and do them within this month.

A Gentle Reminder to Conference Co-ordinators

Ideas are not free, they take time and energy to create, and ideas people such as authors and illustrators should be valued or their work will vanish.

Authors value being asked to speak at conferences and the indirect compliment that their work is appreciated. However, there's concern that conference organisers are assuming authors and illustrators do not need to be paid a fee for presenting their researched talks, nor for their travel or accommodation expenses. It's assumed that a mention of their book as publicity is sufficient. This is not the case.

An author or an illustrator is a self-employed creator in the business of ideas and their intellectual property is available for a fee. Their time must be costed too. Professional conference organisers are paid corporate rates, volunteer-organiser librarians and teachers have salaries, but authors are expected to donate their time and pay registration fees for the privilege of attending.

Sometimes volunteer organisers who are paid a salary for their 'other job' find it difficult to understand that 'writing' and 'speaking' which result in the sale of books are the author's core business. Often volunteer organisers ask 'as a favour' and this makes it difficult for shy authors to insist on payment when there's mutual admiration and an appreciation of working within a budget between authors and librarians and teachers.

Since the authors' ideas or work are the primary conference content and may even form the in-service training for many attendees who pay their registration fee, a proportion of this conference income ought to be allocated to a speaker-author's budget. On the ASA website, suggested minimum speaking fees for authors are listed.

Some organisers pay only travel and accommodation but others expect authors to pay all their own expenses and even the three to four day registration fee which may be hundreds of dollars. Some big publishers pay the expenses of their major authors from their publicity budget and insist their authors' books be available for sale, but writers with smaller or new publishers are not financially supported.

Publishing houses do not pay expenses for authors who publish with more than one company. Author academics have their fees paid by their educational institution, and attend the conference in their 'other' capacity, but this means conference participants miss out on exposure to a range of innovative writers who are full time professional creators and who may publish through new or experimental mediums. Librarians and teachers need to meet these new creators, for the sake of their students/clients and to keep up to date professionally.

Conferences should be seen as benefiting the people who attend, not as free PR for authors. Authors are a resource for ideas and if conference organisers see authors simply as PR machines, that's what they'll get at their conferences – authors who are basically there to sell their books, not to discuss ideas which are relevant to the specific audience.

There's a dilemma for authors dealing with 'well intentioned' but commercially naïve volunteers who say, 'But you'll publicise your books, isn't that enough?' Often books are not available for sale at the conferences, due to volunteer mismanagement or overload.

Mistakenly, conference attendees assume that an author receives the total amount of the book, not the 10% royalty or even less if there are 'special' sales of remaindered copies. For example, if an author signs and sells 100 books, at $10 each they may receive less than $100 for the day's work. Here are some recent specific incidences:

- Author invited 15 months before the conference, to give a major talk based on their forthcoming book, accepted and then found out later they were expected to pay their own interstate travel,accommodation and the registration for the entire conference, which also included their own session for which others were charged a fee.
- Interstate major author told that they would be refunded the cheapest, non-changeable airfare, but they had to leave at a very early hour, unless prepared to pay the difference and find their own booking. Refunded months later.
- Author required to pay a day registration of over $100 to participate in a panel session on a topic subsequently not related to their books, and the titles were neither available in the conference bookshop, nor publicised in any way. Their name was not on the program.
- Authors agreed to speak as a 'freebie' for a country conference out of respect for the author-organiser and then discovered participants were charged, a large profit was made and a massively expensive publicity campaign only gave authors a minor or no billing in comparison with other 'entertainers' who were paid.
- Authors invited to donate their time and skills for a low budget, 'worthy' conference and subsequently finding that participants are charged a high entry and this money is used to pay for accommodation for organisers and their partners, publicity and 'freebies' for entertainers.
- An author who agreed to speak for 'free' on condition that their books were available for sale at their talk, was stopped from autographing and selling their own copies which the bookstore did not carry despite previously having provided a list. There was no return to the out of pocket author who paid their own travel expenses, car parking fee and registration.

Concurrent sessions: Authors who agree to speak, find they are programmed on concurrent sessions where there are so many options, only two or three people arrive or the sessions are cancelled.

Unfair to publishers: A growing trend is for conferences to only invite authors via publishers and then invoice the publishers for fares to be repaid once the author has agreed to speak on an expenses paid basis.

Publishers pay reluctantly afterwards because they do not wish to offend their authors.

Payment for authors of children's and young adult (YA) books and adult writers should be equal for comparable sessions. Examples have been given of conferences where the children's student sessions were incredibly well-attended and subsidied the rest of the festival, but children's authors were paid less for longer sessions.

Speaking suggestions

Priorities: Authors should be aware that organisers may have a limited budget although often this is a matter of priorities. The author-speaker budget should have a higher priority than table decorations, free accommodation for organisers' partners or exotic thematic catering.

Reduce the number of concurrent sessions and focus on the invited speakers who should be paid.

Invite carefully and use the speakers more than once in a conference.

Make sure all their books are available for sale alongside or within walking distance of the conference hall.

Schedule a signing session immediately after the talk.

A minimum requirement is that authors presenting a paper should not pay registration and that all their expenses should be paid.

When invitations are issued, it should be made clear if a fee is available for speakers or panel participants and whether they are expected to pay registration. Often there's up to a year's time lag, so details should be clear. When the conference invitation is offered, if it is made clear that the author will not be paid, and they are still prepared to attend and participate, that is acceptable. It is an informed choice. Well serviced book sales and local media publicity may be worthwhile with a negotiated lower fee for some authors, but they should have the choice.

An academic who writes the occasional book and has a regular salary is often prepared to speak without being paid because their educational institution covers their expenses and registration and it is a 'credit' requirement of their employment. But this means the conference is denied the range of potential speakers if they are limited to those who will work for free. Morally, an ideas person is worthy of their hire for the job they do, not whether they are paid from elsewhere.

Many authors refuse and some are considering not accepting these unpaid 'invitations' in future and peak bodies who organise conferences need to be aware of this.

Authors are a valuable international resource. It is important not to waste them.

> ### Authorpreneurial Hint
>
> Practise accepting/rejecting certain kinds of invitations. Here are five conditions you can negotiate:
>
> - Fee
> - Travel
> - Kinds of publicity
> - Timing and the number of concurrent sessions
> - Availability of (your) books for sale at the venue.

From Local to International

Sponsors, investors or grants

Applying for grants and subsidies can become a full time occupation. Learning the politics of certain groups in order to gain financial or in-kind support can be very time consuming. Therefore, authorpreneurs often invest in themselves and pay their own way in exploratory visits, significant festivals or by providing samples. With emphasis upon the quality of their unique idea and its commercial viability, they may seek sponsors or investors rather than grants. Others try innovations such as crowd funding as a way of attracting pledges of support online.

Providing samples or the obligatory book gifts for exchange, especially in Asia can be a big expense. But providing unprotected eCopies brings with it the worry of piracy. An access code to an online version for a limited period is an alternative to giving samples or review copies.

Academics or those working for large organisations often have the benefit of exposure to innovative practices and contacts during sabbaticals, overseas study visits or paid conferences. However, this may mean there is an ethical dilemma between private and public conflicts of interest and insider trading may exist. It is unfair for tax free, government subsidised projects to compete against quotes from individuals. But it happens, especially in the educational training and literacy area.

Other time-poor creators who are short of money have found innovative ways to profile their work. These include:

- Being involved in a group display or a travelling exhibition.
- Using professional newsletters to keep informed of opportunities.
- Having a benefactor, umbrella organisation or mentor to publicise work.
- Locating international peers who work in a similar fashion and help each other.
- Being interviewed or profiled in international media, (such as blogs or journals or YouTube) with links to the creator's website.
- Sending material with an agent or colleague in lieu of personal attendance.
- Using introductions via the professional organisations to which you belong.

One illustrator explained: It is highly beneficial to be a Society of Children's Book Writers and Illustrators (SCBWI) member when travelling overseas. 'Through the local rep in Paris, I spoke at the American Library in Paris, a school in Bilbao, Spain and attended a great meeting with agents at a SCBWI dinner in New York. I also attended a dinner with other SCBWI members and agents/publishers in New York and London.'

Some international ventures don't lead to immediate book sales. The actual visit may have seemed a waste of time, apart from the scenery and the food. However, following up the contacts and writing about the experience, eventually pays off in unexpected ways. Translation or an offer of film rights might follow a couple of years after a personal visit or a local agent may become interested in your work.

Writing a candid analysis of your personal international process can be beneficial for others. Hints on what not to do or what you've learned from the experience can clarify the issues for you and others and make the next visit more productive. For example, you may discover that 'multi-cultural' for some Americans may mean Latino only. Or that 'international' publishing refers only to those American houses which have editions of books from elsewhere, not international publishers in other countries. Or that many people think Australia is Austria, and are surprised that English is spoken so well as a second language.

Cultural expectations

Do not appear rude, just because you are ignorant of the customs. It pays to research beforehand.

- Use the accepted form of address e.g. be more formal, don't just say 'Hi'.
- Dress appropriately e.g. be guided by your host or interpreter.
- Learn the formal way to present and appreciate business cards.
- Learn the local greeting in their language. Bow if appropriate.
- Pay for excess baggage to bring home business gifts.
- Carry 'light' gifts to give, preferably your autographed books.
- Toasting: Say you are 'teetotal' so you can respond to the numerous toasts with non-alcoholic drinks.
- Always praise the surroundings or food of your hosts.
- Get your business card and proposals translated.
- Prepare printed handouts in dual languages.
- Only discuss business after the pleasantries. Follow the lead of the host.
- It is often difficult to judge whether it was a 'yes', 'no' or 'maybe'.
- Write emails in simple English and in short sentences.
- The logistics of getting international book supplies on time are often complicated by customs, taxes or bribes and whether someone 'knows' an official. Occasionally, works are pulped or confiscated by a censor or large taxes are added.
- Wording on customs labels can be crucial. Whether you state your package is a gift or sample, as well as your estimate of the value, can affect whether the books get through. It is often assumed that multiple copies of your book are for commercial sale rather than as samples or gifts.

Commercial Hints

- Gold medal stickers on covers sell books internationally. Non-readers use these as an indication of whether the work is worthy of investment if an award has been won.
- Classics and film-linked books attract attention.
- An author website is a vital resource for potential foreign buyers.

- Order business cards in bulk and use them. It is more efficient to collect others in sequence.
- Use the face recognition ID for photographs on iPhoto, especially when names are very similar.

Interpreters and Translators

- If giving a talk, use visuals, and speak slowly. Allow the interpreter time to express your thoughts.
- Supply the text of the talk beforehand for the interpreter to prepare, and keep to the sequence.
- Include a map, and explain the basics of where you came from and your family etc.
- Use a map to show the distance between your home and your talk city.
- Respond to the face of the speaker, not the interpreter.
- Simplify but on no account use colloquialisms.

Make use of the setting you have visited in your next book. But check with a local that you have portrayed customs appropriately. Use naïve (for story only) and expert (for facts) readers for double checking.

Authorpreneurial Hint

Initiate contact with an international publisher or producer. And follow up, politely.

3: Authorpreneurial Tips and Tricks

Proposals Rather than Gambles

Writing a proposal is a multi-purpose undertaking, forcing you to consider the market and structure of your future book, series or project. A proposal also changes publication from a gamble to a better possibility of gaining investment for a business plan.

Check what else is around in your chosen field. Find out in what way yours will be better or different.

If nothing else exists, decide if that is because there is no market, or because you are innovative.

What niche will your idea fill? Does it suit a genre? Is it un/like a well known title? Search online, cruise bookshops and research publishers.

List ten possible publishers/markets and start at the top. Simultaneous submission is acceptable if you tell them. Alternatively offer for a month and then if you haven't heard from them by then, indicate you will assume they are not interested and you'll move to the next on your list.

Decide in what kinds of formats you will offer this proposal: print, digital, manual, 'how to', fiction, faction or case-studies? And for what period: two years or will it be negotiable annually?

How will you research it and how will you cover the costs? Find out if seeding money is available.

You might also consider co-writing with an expert in this field.

Collect relevant organisational support for your project like a letter suggesting members would buy this. How many members belong to the organisation? Will they underwrite part of the print run?

Structure your project around the most common questions/problems and provide strategies for answering or solving these.

Is your expertise academic or industrial or participant-observer (you've done it while gathering data)? Or are you a naïve newcomer who typifies the reader and asks beginner questions?

What is your track record of previous publication or performance? Is it in this area or in another field? What's the relevance?

Is your proposal topical? Could it, for instance, be linked to an anniversary?

A one page proposal is a strict discipline, but it should be most persuasive to convince your chosen publisher(s) that the project is viable, when written by you.

For fiction, include a one page synopsis, for non-fiction, a table of contents.

To save time, both yours and that of the publisher, prepare well. Just providing the answers, will force you to plan your project more realistically and convince the publisher the project is viable. Alternately, of course, it may convince you – that it is not!

What you will need/Contents of a proposal

- Why there is a need for this book. Is it topical?
- Your name and contact details
- Job, experience and qualifications relevant to project
- Previous publications
- Proposed title (and sub-title)
- Scope of project
- Table of contents
- Length (in approximate wordage)
- Manuscript delivery date
- Market (potential readers, curriculum links)
- Unique features of the project
- Competition list
- Strengths and weaknesses of competition
- Why your book might be better than what's already available.

Contract: Your aim is to get a publishing contract with an advance and royalties based on at least 10% of the recommended retail price (RRP) with rising royalties after a certain number of sales. The publisher will cover costs of publishing, distribution and marketing.

Simultaneous submission means you offer the concept on a non-exclusive basis and decide on the best offer. Other options may include collaborative publishing, where you pay some of the costs.

Query email: This is a mini-proposal and should be brief. Only send it if email queries are acceptable to this market.

Cover Letter: For a picture book, the cover letter should be simple, as the manuscript text will accompany it. You will need to adapt this as relevant for non-fiction or other genres. Check publisher or agent website for submission details.

- Get the right person/editor's name/title to address snail mail or email if arranged beforehand.
- Enclosed is my (insert length e.g. 32-page picture book) text (insert title) which is aimed at (insert target audience e.g. teen/toddlers/primary/adult) which explores the issue of (insert themes e.g. child/grandparent relationships/eco-systems/pets).
- No illustrations are included but the style of (reference style) appeals to me for this story because (insert reason e.g. can draw children realistically/has knowledge of machines etc).
- This story is based on my experience as a (insert experience e.g. swimming instructor/mountain guide/trainer) and has been trialled with appropriately aged children.
- The subject is topical because (insert reason e.g. 2024 is the International Year of …).
- My previous publications include (insert summary of literary CV e.g. mainly short stories and articles in magazines).
- I'm aware that you get many submissions, but this manuscript fits your list because (insert reason which indicates you've done your research of their latest catalogue).

A proposal will be written before the book exists, but sometimes a publisher may request a sample chapter to check the writing style. It's wise to have a draft first chapter available.

If the proposal is unsuccessful, don't write the book! Re-write the proposal.

> **Authorpreneurial Hint**
>
> Draft a proposal for your next project by the end of this week, and submit it.

Pitching for Business

As an authorpreneur you're more likely to be initiating and so you may be 'pitching' a new process or concept as well as the content. If using terms which are new to your audience, keep it simple. Don't assume they know all the new verbs of how to do something technical, that you've just learnt recently.

Pitchathon: Be convincing as to why your project is saleable/publishable now. Practise to a time limit, even to the dog! Say it to a mirror or record it.

Speed Dating: Some publishers host bookseller events at which that season's list authors have a limited time in which to explain why their book is relevant. Booksellers rotate in five minute slots around the author tables, ask questions and give feedback on what appeals to their markets. At the end, orders are placed with the publisher on titles which have convinced them. In anticipation of next season, list six points on why your book or project may appeal. You're permitted to use visuals such as the cover.

Chances are your project will cross media. Practise with the equipment, so there are no technical hitches.

Humour helps, if it is relevant. For example, one illustrator presented a fast, humorous autobiography in book covers they had designed. But it was the wit of their comments, which convinced future clients of the depth of her ideas and flexibility.

Consider the project from the listener's perspective. What do they most need from you?

Play Devil's Advocate. Point out the likely problems and how you will solve them with your innovation. For example, challenges of adult literacy could be addressed through simple performance scripts and reading with a purpose. In remote regions eScripts are excellent for easy accessibility.

Where would this project fit within their existing list? Show you have researched them.

A creator profile and CV are different. Indicate your relevant skills for this project. A CV is where you have been. A profile indicates what you can do.

List non-traditional markets: Consider three possible markets for your current project.

Time lag: It may be a good idea, but in the wrong place at the wrong time. Despite fear of imitation, leave your proposal on file with the producer. Often your current proposal may remind them when they are seeking new writers for another series.

Prepare a very well presented folder with samples and contact links for later study, especially if any translation or costings are involved. Non-native speakers may need to have your words translated and their significance considered.

Flexibility: Be willing to re-structure according to clients' current budgets or requirements, but build in payment stages, rather than working on speculation.

Rates and conditions: Inform yourself of industry rates and don't undercut yourself. Decide whether to risk a percentage of eventual profits: (gross and net are significantly different) or take a fee now and no continuing interest. Do you want this to enhance your reputation? Is it crucial to have your name included or is it for a charity?

Track record: Give examples of previously completed projects. Copyright your material and keep evidence of dated, earlier drafts.

Investigate trade marking or patents if appropriate.

Collaborative projects: Clarify rights and have signed agreements on expenses and income splits.

Time frame: Some projects such as animation or film take years, and others never get past the initial stages. It is important to stagger your projects, so you are not living on hopes.

If this concept is emotionally significant to you, the financial considerations may be secondary. But you need to monitor how much time and energy can be given long-term.

Authorpreneurial Hint

Pitch a proposal this week in a way you haven't tried before.

Finances, Agents and Legal Stuff

Agents

- Do you need one? Factors here include whether an agent considers you worth representing and whether your output justifies their attention. Some publishers claim to deal only through agents.
- An agent is paid to work on your behalf because they are skilled at presenting apt material to publishers or they have the appropriate international contacts. Specialised agents have different roles. A literary agent charges 10-15%, negotiates contracts, initiates work and handles rights. A speakers' agency takes bookings for talks. A PR agency may be contracted just for the launch of one book. Some agents perform all roles.
- Agented material can jump the 'slush' pile, but so can work of well known writers. Agents specialise in publishing opportunities for their clients because their main job is keeping up to date and many creators prefer to concentrate on writing as their core business. Agents' recommendations within their client base mean extra work across projects in which they have writers and directors etc and direct access to festivals.
- Using an agent separates 'business' negotiation from artistic decisions, especially for shy or busy creators. Many agents have relationships with peers in New York, London and other centres and may split some fees. An agent acts on your financial behalf, but also carries your reputation.
- Check if a prospective agent belongs to the agents' professional society and agrees to their code of conduct. Ensure that this agent is legally qualified to handle contracts and rights management.

These are the major areas in which writers generally need help.

- Options: Learn relevant contract law, choose a publisher with an active translation and rights department who sell within their own subsidiaries and attend international book rights fairs, or rely on contract advice from professional writers' organisations. The size of advances and rising royalty clauses or careful subsidiary rights negotiations can make the difference between a full time work style as a writer and keeping your day job.

- An agent has a continuing financial interest in contracts negotiated for his/her authors, which is why authors with big backlists rarely divorce their agents.
- Be wary of 'dodgy' online sites that claim to be agents. No legitimate agent charges a 'reading fee'. These are often vanity publishing sites, seeking clients to pay for all costs of publication, with no distribution or quality control. Trade agents who claim commissions or fees for 'advice' or translation may also be dodgy. Consider contacting agents who are members of the Australian Literary Agents' Association, which has a Code of Practice.
- Having an agent is not necessarily a way of reducing paperwork. You may still have to monitor contracts and be aware of business transaction and tax implications.
- A speakers' agency handles bookings for talks and accepts fees on your behalf, which should be forwarded immediately, less their agreed commission. So it is in their interest to generate more work for you. However, if the agents' reputation is poor, this will also reflect on the reputation of the author.

Professional Organisations

Belonging to professional organisations is an investment in professional updating of skills, legal support, networking and political lobbying for arts trade issues such as PLR, ELR and copyright. It is tax deductible as well. But the real value is not feeling alone if something with massive financial implications goes wrong or even goes spectacularly right.

Contracts

Copy your contract agreements and file them in two different places. Bushfires, flood and other natural disasters can occur. Check also that you retain a copy or digital copy of the contracts signed by both parties. Often a contract is returned to a publisher for the second witness or signature and isn't returned, so when there's a query about rights, there's a problem. If collaborating, have an agreement about rights splits between collaborators too. The ASA offers contract assessments for members. Use it or seek legal advice elsewhere.

Are you a hoarder or de-clutterer? Consider donating manuscript drafts and associated book paperwork or memorabilia to literary archives.

There are tax implications too, if they are donated in bulk rather than in dribs and drabs.

Invoices and tax, BAS, GST, cash flow: It's useful to have a generic invoice available for easy issue which contains contacts details, GST, Business Number and the electronic accounts to which you wish to be paid. (Keep these accounts with small balances or use PayPal or similar.)

Do you need an accountant, a book keeping service or a computer program for accounts? Find out what services colleagues are using and whether you could share them. Does your professional organisation offer any extra services like mentoring?

New creators' businesses have mainly outgoings. Most aim to move from amateur part time to full time in about five years. Big fluctuations of income can occur and so it's wise to spread income, as primary producers do, across three years. Or to have a two to three day a week 'bread and butter' job.

Investing means you hope to gain long-term benefit, otherwise it's mismanagement or gambling. For the self-employed creator it's wise to get some tax advice. Which big items are viable in your business plan?

- Is a more appropriate vehicle to carry your 'tools of trade' viable?
- Do you need to 'up-skill' by doing a course or paying for assistance? Relying on 'swapping' skills or when a family member has time to 'do it for free', can mean lost opportunities and tension.
- Is an international conference fee a good investment in networking for jobs? (Or only if you're also on the program as a speaker?)
- Since creators earn minimal amounts with occasional windfalls, management of intellectual property may be crucial long-term because an 'old' work may have another life, in a new format or an international market. Is the time and cost involved in preparing a high quality sample, a good investment?

Making a profit

Calculate on an annual rather than a weekly basis. Concentrate on more in, than out. Money is measurable but for an artist, reputation and winning awards may also translate into sales and future work.

Self-publishing for many authors can be extremely expensive. Unless you have good distribution, paying for editing and printing may be a bad investment. Do a detailed costing on a business plan first, even for a family history and especially for fiction. Obtain quotes from a number of publishing services providers and compare costs. It may be cheaper to use ePublishing but various middle people take percentages from naïve clients, and some formats restrict sales to certain markets. Ensure that you understand the terms of your agreement with the publishing services provider before you sign it or pay your deposit. Seek advice from the ASA or another organisation if you have any concerns.

Insurance

Check whether you need public liability for your home workplace, or disability insurance to cover injury time. Several artists in bushfire or flood prone areas have lost original works, which are uninsurable and not replaceable.

Various management courses advocate the SMART approach to goal setting:

- Specific
- Measurable
- Attainable
- Realistic
- Time bound.

Or use the KISS method – Keep It Simple Stupid. The solution is a balance between actually producing original material and effectively evaluating what you are doing and the income.

For example, Writer A attends many workshops and all literary festivals, buys motivational eBooks, 'invests' in every computer program relating to plotting and time management, makes lists, graphs their 'creative' time and talks about the novel they are going to write once their 'writer's block' is overcome. 'Creative Writing' is an excuse to avoid all other household tasks, especially changing the baby's nappy. Writer B writes for two hours every day or 1,000 words, whichever occurs first, with the aim of finishing the book length manuscript before their significant birthday. Which writer gets your vote as more likely to succeed?

Legal stuff for writers includes rights management, copyright, plagiarism and fear of being sued by disgruntled family or ex-lovers who identify themselves in fictional characters. Keep records you can find in a hurry.

Beginning writers often fear their concepts or good ideas will be stolen if they submit them to large organisations as a series proposal. This is unlikely but it's wise not to tell all without some agreement or recompense.

Plagiarism is knowingly copying parts of another's work and presenting it as your own original work. Students sometimes do it, which is the ultimate compliment but illegal. Realistically it's likely that dramatic events like bushfires/floods will stimulate creative minds to write similar stories, so several creators may work from the same stimuli and produce similar stories such as fictional disappearances or mistaken identity around disaster settings.

Occasionally books are pulped because of complaints by those in close relationships to the author. Ironically they often complain they are the character that is the unpleasant one. Arts Law Centre of Australia can offer legal advice, as can the Copyright Agency Limited.

In-kind payment instead of income/money: Applying to visit extreme locations and use the setting in future books is a way some creators research and take a holiday simultaneously. They also might offer to write for an organisation in exchange for publicity or experiences.

Sales, Marketing and More

Merchandising

Some sites offer licensing of illustrations on T-shirts, mugs etc. These are mainly relevant for illustrators or cartoonists.

Gifts of the imagination: Offering writing skills in kind for specific people. Examples include product placement of a name as a character offered at charity auction or lyrics of a birthday song.

Richness of life may be a compensation for big superannuation for some writers who live the daily working life others aim for in retirement.

> **Authorpreneurial Hint**
>
> Update your rights-reverted file. Duplicate records of contracts, in 'e' and print format, and file them in different places.

Travel, Time and Energy Management

Lawyers have chargeable minutes for their advice and time. Writers don't, but author travel is work. So, travel and energy management is vital for an authorpreneur who has to manage their own schedule and who is often expected to give free advice at awkward moments in transit. An example is:

> I have this great idea for a book, but I'm just too busy to get the time to write it. What do you advise?

Distinguish between acknowledging a genuine fan or fan mail and being asked for extensive 'freebie' manuscript assessment or personal recommendations. Refer these requests to professional organisations or have links available on your website for 'Aspiring Writers' or a generic sheet of advice.

Analyse your past year. How many long work trips did you make?

Which were satisfying and if so why? Examples include:

- Well organised and fulfilled goals
- Fun
- Back-up at home made it possible
- Income
- Contacts for future projects

Which were not satisfying and why?

- Away too long, beyond optimum charm rate (four days for one author)
- Lack of book sales or lost opportunities
- Wasted time due to bad planning
- Fatigue or frustration meant unproductive day on return
- Still had to maintain other projects, on the run, while in transit
- Couldn't use new electronics effectively to keep in touch

Strategic Conferences

If you're invited to give a keynote, your negotiated fee and expenses are covered. But often author-speakers are not paid. Academics who are authors get double value. As mentioned earlier, apart from being on a salary, academic speaker-authors' expenses to attend professional conferences are funded by their institutions. Publishers recommend their A list authors and often have to pay their conference expenses, but this is linked to a book release as part of the publicity cost.

Self-employed writers have to fund themselves and pay the daily conference fee! Consequently, you may decide this conference is not worth the investment for you, unless your work is reaching new markets.

Requests for 'recording' your conference sessions for future unlimited use is an issue for an authorpreneur who is 'selling' original ideas. You can suggest additional fees for this recording, or offer in lieu, a link to where your book or information is sold in multi-media formats.

If you're starting out, being a panelist in the program is a form of advertising.

- Will you learn enough to make the cost of attending this conference worthwhile at your stage?
- Are you viewing attendance as a holiday from working alone?
- What income are you losing by being there?
- Will your books be available for sale in a strategic time or place? Will others know that?

Incurring Financial Rates

Insisting on payment makes you less attractive to the conference organisers compared to 'free' speakers in your field. Check how many concurrent sessions are being held or you may not have an audience. Check ASA suggested rates. Badly organised festivals are great time wasters, causing frustration for the self-employed with considerable costs for little financial return but selective appearances on strategic programs can be advantageous.

Value-adding: Try to add paid employment or research in the local area to offset costs. Or offer to do a conference web chat from your home office as a PR novelty.

Fatigue counts as a cost if one day's paid work effectively takes three day's effort. If airfares are covered by your host, they may book very early or late flights which are cheaper for their budget, but inconvenient and fatiguing with 4.30am starts and midnight finishes. It may be viable to upgrade at your own cost or pay the difference for flights at reasonable hours, so you can work at home. Or make use of airline clubs, which offer working space and refreshment.

Managing Travel

If booking your own flights, allow leeway in flight connections to reduce stress, and allow for different time zones. Plan to do follow up administration en route home or just 'chill out' and accept that you need rest after a heavy schedule, or decide on the day, depending on fatigue or your energy level.

Travel with colleagues. It's more sociable and you can share costs and take the opportunity to update, en route. Remember to respect those who prefer quiet 'time out' if you're travelling in a group.

Some consultants book more expensive flexible fares on certain 'legs' in case plans are changed, or they need to arrive refreshed. They then take cheap 'red eye' specials at other times or to allow for the flight on which they need more baggage allowance. Paying a night's accommodation can be expensive or it can be an investment. As a way of life, working in the fog of no sleep is counter-productive.

Carry-on luggage can speed exits from your arrival airport but excess baggage is a problem for those carrying heavy books. Arrange for your publisher to mail books to the destination host. For an author, books and large character props are 'tools of trade', but check beforehand. Don't take more than you can carry yourself. Murphy's Law states that the room where you speak will be furthest from the car park so always use bags on wheels.

Long-term airport parking: Frequent travellers disagree about whether it is better to park close in A or B and be last on and off the long-term bus or walk. Others prefer to park further out at X Y Z and be the first to load their bags and get a seat. All agree it is expensive but not as much as taxis or getting partners to collect/chauffeur at odd hours.

For regional areas, a train may be more relaxing and allow you to work en route. However, your own car provides you with an already packed mobile car office, especially if you wish to sell heavy books. You can listen to audio books while driving and keep up to date with radio interviews, news etc.

Clothing: Take the minimum and restrict yourself to drip-dry with layers for changing climates. If you are likely to be photographed, use scarves or shirts for colour variety. Wear comfortable shoes and an all purpose, tailored jacket to look 'professional'.

Streamline: Co-ordinate interstate travel with two or three events in the one area but nothing conflicting with your host's wishes or audiences. Ensure you are electronically available for last minute media.

Collate generic travel details on one file for hosts. These can include Frequent Flyer numbers, ABN (Australian Business Number), GST registered, Working With Children Check form and insurance numbers with your website, mobile and landline. You may also choose to add a bio and bibliography. Indicate electronic payment preferences and when you expect an invoice to be paid: on the day or at another time?

Charm by-pass: Fatigue is common on work travel due to mental and physical stimulation but also from the need to be constantly charming. Pace yourself by building in time to follow your hobbies or exercise locally. One author is an op-shop vintage collector. Another photographs country towns for on-going projects. A third naps.

There's novelty value about a stranger visiting. Use the associated publicity opportunities before, during and after your visit. List forthcoming events on your website, with links to host websites to help them too (always assure potential burglars that someone else lives in your house while you're away working on those dates). Read the local newspaper and watch local television when visiting and make local references in your talks to the football team's name or fortunes for instance.

Plan next year after analysing what worked this time, or add notes to never do this again!

Serendipity: This is the unexpected, joyful benefit. Often if you make the extra effort to visit in person or do more than your share, even if the project makes no money, you often learn something worthwhile, unexpectedly. There is real pleasure when this happens because you decide to finish the project to a high standard regardless, to satisfy your own sense of professionalism. But if you toil on alone, and this happens too often, you need to reassess how you choose projects and the amount of travel involved.

Daily exercise is vital for mental endurance and to increase energy levels. Writing broadens the mind, but also broadens the bottom if you sit too much.

> ## Authorpreneurial Hint
>
> Apply the one extra task per day approach. For the self-employed who can allocate their own time, deciding priorities is crucial.
>
> Should you do the things you prefer or those which can be finished quickly and give a sense of accomplishment, or slowly tackle the 'bigger' jobs which affect the skills you will need long-term to survive as a business? Decide and act.

Confidence, Success and Reputation

Self-confidence is without a doubt a big issue for those not yet published but also for those who have had initial success and are not confident they can produce something comparable, ever again. Accept that this afflicts others, at all stages: beginners, those in mid-career and the highly experienced.

As many creators work alone, maintaining confidence in the quality and output of work is a challenge, especially on a long project. Be aware of any pattern in 'feeling down' or loss in confidence at certain times of the year or stages in the work process. Acknowledge to yourself that qualms of confidence are part of the process.

Some creators are 'responsive' personalities who work best to an outside deadline or an intriguing proposal. They are likely to 'procrastinate' if no outside stimulus is available. January is a 'slow' time for the self-employed and if little stimulation is coming from outside markets, it's wise to build in other forms of motivation.

Start with the easiest or the shortest, and keep going. Try to complete a task, even if a small one. This promotes the self-confidence that you can complete even big jobs, which in effect are simply compilations of smaller tasks.

Do you see colleagues as competitors? Developing two to three peers with whom to share ideas is helpful, as long as they are not potential competitors.

Collaborative projects have built-in obligations, and deadlines, but also the opportunity for mutual support.

Confidence can be eroded by family and/or friends who 'trivialise' the creative process and judge your ability and success only by money paid for a final 'product'. Avoid such 'negative' people, even if they live in your house.

Anticipation of public rejection cripples some creators. Scared of public appraisal of their work, they prefer to keep it as a work in progress (WiP), with the excuse that they know it is less than perfect but they will fix it up eventually. Just as a parent must let a child 'go', so must a writer allow the manuscript to be independent and stand alone.

Are your critics objective or subjective? Look at the reasons given by critics and if their suggestions are relevant, apply them to your next project.

Brashness, over-confidence and too much 'I-I-I' is a turn-off. There's a fine line between following up politely two or three times and being a pest. The ease of social media can make constant sales suggestions via email or Twitter alienating.

Distinguish between fatigue and sub-standard work or artistic dissatisfaction affecting your confidence. Exercise, rest and eat healthily. Then tackle emotional patterns affecting confidence. Maybe you know the work isn't good enough and that's what is really sapping your confidence. All creators have favourite creations, which may not be popular choices with the public. Meanwhile, some of their lesser skilled works may attract greater prestige and attention and earn more. Don't be self-deprecating and 'put down' your popular works. Accept compliments graciously.

Keep a list of what worked well, and revisit these when you feel 'down'.

Success is achievement of your aims. Publication or performance, income and hours spent are not the only form of evaluation.

Confidence comes from skills achieved and then acknowledgement by others. Recognition and respect by your peers is a version of success.

Ego-Googling or checking on mentions of your projects via Google Alerts and so on is a monitoring technique but avoid developing an over-reliance on it.

Updating your Creative CV, which stresses skills, can affect confidence. Include your CV with proposals. Updating bios and bibliographies can remind you of how much you have done. Also take a look at other writers' sample CVs as often they have similar skills but have expressed them differently or more effectively.

How you feel and what you have achieved are two different categories of success or failure: subjective and objective. But 'reputation' rests on others' evaluations of you. Remember that liking and competence are not the same.

Taking time out to discuss the implications or significance of your project can be coupled with exercise with a colleague. Walk while you talk, especially if you are at a conference or working away from home or 'out of' routine.

Don't forget that success is relative. A beginner writer may consider publication is the height of their ambition. A mid-career author may consider a publicity circuit with a book launch and a film option is success. An experienced author may want blocks of uninterrupted time to do quality work. And a genuine fan letter saying how much reading that book meant personally is success!

Confidence will rise and fall in a creator. The only reassurance is that having been 'down' and 'up', you know it is possible for the situation to reverse. It is that confidence which will enable you to keep working, despite external critics and few markets or internal doubts.

Authorpreneurial Hint

What gave you a confidence or a financial boost? Re-create those circumstances.

Speaking Circuits

Name any talk or workshop you give by the title of your book. Link it to your website or where the book is available for sale. Tell audiences more than once you have books.

Base a flexible talk around the letters of a key word in your title e.g. 'Antarctica'. Have a main point for each letter, in case you get nervous. A mnemonic format, which can be adapted to your latest project, is:

AUTHOR

A for Anecdote or Aim of the book.

U for Understanding, or how it was researched.

T for significance of Title

H for Humour

O for Originality

R for Re-writing or the process of drafting

Prepare a sequence of visuals, but change the sophistication of the 'how I work' talk according to your audience. A mixed audience of adults, adolescents, pre-teens and babies is the hardest. Build in a couple of fun activities. Most are interested in the process by which a book is created and what went wrong!

Don't read long extracts especially if you write poetry but do leave time for questions. A good idea is to offer an incentive prize for the most imaginative question.

Carry business cards, and bookmarks showing your website details, plus ISBNs of your other books so the audience can find/buy them later. Autograph books or bookmarks only, not bits of paper which get lost.

Props are useful for photographs, but only if they are related to your book and not too heavy. Allowable 'tools of trade' on a plane may not attract excess baggage charges.

Build in tactile, aural, visual, smells and tastes if possible so that you appeal to all. For example, offer a sample of hard ship's biscuits from the historic period of your book.

If you are a beginner, you'll often be asked to speak for free, with a gift pen or flowers or a bottle of wine if you're a bloke.

Once experienced, you need to state your speaking fee. If you find this difficult, just state you charge ASA rates and refer them to the ASA website. Travel and accommodation are extra. Once you reach the keynote conference status, you can charge your suggested fee.

Naïve but pleasant hosts suggest the opportunity to sell your books should be sufficient recompense for your talk. Explain you'd need to sell at least 40 books to make the hourly rate of most teachers. Remember that time speaking is time away from writing, which is your core business.

Some speakers have the alternative viewpoint that speaking is their core business, and the books and audio sales are extras.

Despite many creators being shy personalities, the ability to speak on radio, TV or give talks increases the chances of selling your books. Carry some with you but if there's a local bookseller, support them.

Display your books with your front 'working' copy with sticker showing price and three to four others behind it for sale. Use a 'damaged' (stained with coffee or wine or wrongly signed) book as your speaking (not for sale) copy.

Carry business cards, bookmarks, your bio and a list of books or quotes for any journalists wanting interviews. Use your camera to get a digital shot for later publicity. Have an autographing pen, which flows well. A speaker's book bag on wheels, which contains electronic leads, sample books, posters and a cash float, should be manageable by you alone, as 'minders' are not always available.

Double-check the location, time and contact persons as some institutions have multiple campuses and your invitation may have come from the other one.

Service clubs have honorary speaker secretaries who change annually, so ask for confirmation a week before. There is nothing more frustrating than turning up for a 'freebie' talk to find they've forgotten, moved or double booked. If given a choice of time slot, choose a pre-meal time, as audiences tend to nod off afterwards.

Speakers' agencies charge a commission and may demand exclusivity but may also streamline arrangements for you. The event organiser should carry public indemnity insurance and unless you are giving professional advice, professional indemnity insurance is not needed for an author-speaker.

Distinguish between a publicity talk related to a just released book, and being a speaker as the entertainment. The ASA suggests speaking rates and travel expenses for different kinds of events.

Clarify the technical support you will need. Do they have a microphone? Is there someone who can link the laptop to their system and has the appropriate password? Weekends and out of hours, keys and passwords are the greatest challenges for visiting speakers.

Charitable talks should be your decision and not demanded of you. Of course most authors speak as a donation for their child's school, friends' or their favourite charity. But being asked to donate autographed books to 'auctions' and to post at your own cost, and sometimes not even receive an acknowledgement is a definite no. The most difficult ones to refuse are when the organiser is genuine, and the charity is worthy.

Web chats are a way of offering speaking to regional or remote communities without travel and accommodation costs to hosts. The ASA has a suggested web chat rate too. Videoing should not be done without an additional fee and your right to check the quality, as that talk is your IP.

Authorpreneurial Hint

Prepare a range of talks with your scale of fees attached. Publicise this.

Structuring Public Speaking with Fewer Hassles

Public speaking worries some creators. Whether it's your first time, or you're getting frequent invitations, it helps to have a generic 'talk' shape, which can be adapted to a specific audience.

Use the letters of a key word as the structure for a 'generic' talk. Have three to four 'generic' talks including:

- Humorous autobiographical: including tips for new writers.
- Stages of a book: from idea to publication.
- Genre requirements. For example, how to write scientifically, pace romantically or plot mysteries and use your writing as the example.
- Visuals only, so you can adjust the style or level of comments according to the needs of the audience. Examples would be adult scientists or a pre-school child audience.
- Have a witty ending such as a recipe for a book.

Master Cook Recipe for Getting Published

Quality, fresh ingredients from real life. Mixed story worth telling.

Take out ego and insert craft. Add a sense of humour.

Mixed fruit of adjectives (use moderately). Spice with candid observation.

Balance savoury and sweet. Scatter facts.

Sprinkle anecdotes.

Taste-test with sample readers. Trial various formats.

Add title.

Slow food cooker or microwave? Don't have a kitchen tantrum, insist on others bowing to your misunderstood genius nor write a celebrity cook book. Instead, mould for your intended reader and decorate with PR puff. The result will be a satisfied reader or indigestion due to over-much hot air.

Here's today's Master Cook recipe for Publishing Success:

- Start with fresh, quality ideas
- Add candid insights + anecdotes
- Season with humour
- Blend in research + a title
- Let story rise in moderate oven
- Serve to publishers when ready

Plan B. If you're running late due to traffic, the host's equipment doesn't work or the surrounds/group differ from the brief, it helps if you can talk without any aids.

Consider what your particular type of audience wants to hear: information or entertainment? Are you expected to perform or to share your experiences? Always adjust to your audience's needs. They may be hard of hearing or need facts about Antarctic jobs etc.

Often creators are shy people who work in solitary studios and then have to perform in large public places with hi-tech equipment and big audiences of strangers who are sometimes critics. It's sensible to 'practise' on smaller, friendly groups prior to a publicity tour.

Get fit. Increase your stamina, like an athlete in training, as loss of voice is common on speaking circuits. Be assertive in asking for a microphone, water or refuse to speak over crowds who chat among themselves or noisy bands thumping in nearby tents.

Overlap: If you speak often in the same geographic or interest area or you are recorded nationally, chances are your audience will have heard you before. Change or update your talks and anecdotes at least annually and don't accept groups that overlap.

Electronic challenges: Ask beforehand what equipment is available when you need items such as a data projector. Passwords are often a problem, so check that a password holder is available. For weekend or after-hours, when you are in strange venues, get the mobile number of security and of the 'techie' so you don't get locked in or out.

Have your carry-on airline talks bag on wheels, with backup leads, plugs, markers, name tag stickers etc so you are self-sufficient. Check that these are all returned to you. Buying replacement laptop links can be expensive and they look generic if someone else packs up for you.

It's useful to have a laminated, fold-up giant book cover for a poster or author name or website sign to indicate the location for autographing. This forms a good background for photos too.

Carry book covers in eFormats or utilise host technology to access your website via a whiteboard during talks.

Carry small or extra big props humorously linked to book or research. Suggest a hosts' photograph, and provide a caption for local newspaper or newsletter.

Autographing: Sign only books or bookmarks and ensure you have a different signature from your credit card. Check on the spelling of the name to go in a book. Clarify whether it's a gift for another or for the buyer. Sign after the book has been paid for.

Any accidents with red wine or coffee are your cost. The damaged book will become your demonstration copy and you don't need too many of those!

Allow time for questions as this is often the most enjoyable time. If there are no questions, be ready with some of your own which relate to your next project. You could ask the audience what they would like to have included or offer to share your 'killer' question. What is the question you would least like to be asked? And what is your answer?

Prepare a generic bio sheet (in big print) to offer the ill-prepared host as an introduction and have an extra print copy with you for instant interviews with local journalists. Murphy's Law is that they'll always want a photo and interview mid-talk or when you are autographing. A fact sheet PR business card with website helps to reduce stress, both yours and theirs.

Have books for sale with the price indicated. Usually a flat amount like $20 is easier to administer for change than $19.95. Have change, and investigate whether it's viable to have a credit card machine. Use a book media release as a handout as this has the ISBN, price and available bookstores included.

Powerpoint presentations: Don't just 'read' notes from a screen. Use these aids for visuals such as quirky or informative photos of the writing process.

Repeating yourself! If you are on a PR tour or literary festival, you may have several similar groups and reach the exhaustion stage where you are unable to remember whether you've already used that anecdote with that group. Try to be flexible in using the 'shape' of your talk, but make each talk original. Aim for different kinds of interest groups or talks on the same day.

Pace. Have three or four versatile activities (related to your book), which can be included whenever interest is flagging. Examples include, observation skills for a mystery in which you ask the audience to close their eyes or test their Occupational Health and Safety skills by asking how many exits in the room. A 'generic' talk is a framework to reduce your stress; it should not be boring for them or for you. Use humour.

Authorpreneurial Hint

Listen to an audio or clip of your talk, even if you find it embarrassing. What were two strengths and one weakness? Remedy the weakness next time.

Speed Dating: Titles for Stories or Projects

Matching a title to a story is a vital skill for a writer. A title is the first clue to the story. Either do this before or after you've written the story. Often for eBooks, the title and cover are the only clues. Name each chapter and take the best for the book title.

Try these Speed Dating Title Hints:

Write down three one-word titles; three two-word titles; three three-word titles; and three four-word titles.

Think of colours and write titles related to colours. (three minutes)

Think of emotions and write titles related to emotions. (three minutes)

Jot down three titles containing your character's name.

List three important, message bearing words or phrases from your story.

List three titles of published books, plays, or films that you like. Adapt them as springboards for your own (different) title. Tweak them. Add a 'not' or an 'un'.

Try out your 'best' title on an audience for your story.

Re-use that title for any talks in connection with the book and make a link to where it is available for sale.

Say the title aloud. Is it easy or tongue twisting, or do the words run together and have a second meaning you did not intend?

Trial with the specific audience, just in case 'insiders' have a specific objection.

> **Authorpreneurial Hint**
>
> Check online to see if your title has already been used.

Collaboration

Today, many successful works are not solo efforts. Co-writing is common, as experts collaborate with writers in scientific or medical fields, or when technical expertise is required to structure and idea in new formats. Writers, musicians, graphic designers, animators, puppeteers, technicians, actors, photographers, illustrators and editors are part of the mix.

Collaboration is like a marriage. Some work, others end in literary divorce. Then there is the issue of who owns what. Make sure you clarify rights at the beginning of a project and get a signed agreement between collaborators as well as the contract with the publisher. This should cover even uninvented, multi-media formats.

International collaboration (provided you have a common language or translator) is no more difficult on email or video call, than a face to face working relationship. When there are multiple contributors to one project, they can live anywhere, even in different time zones.

Multiple drafts are a problem so agree on a code for files, or that your collaborator will not add anything until the master copy is returned. Or use the iCloud! Different time zones can be an asset because the writing partner can be working while the others sleeps.

A similar work ethic is vital. Do they deliver on deadlines or do they participate in so many projects that yours is not a high priority? Agree on a timeline, working backwards from the due date.

Are your skills complementary and will you agree to defer to the others' expertise? Decide who will write the final version or whether the roles will be split so that, for example, one does all the business and speaks in the media.

Do you have very different writing styles where one uses long sentences with big words and the other writes concisely? Unless you agree on a procedure, you can waste a lot of time re-working the style to get a compromise.

If we wanted to eat the cake, we had to collaborate to succeed.

Agree on a structure, such as a table of contents, or synopsis and whether you will write together, or cover certain sections individually. Alternatively, one may provide the expert knowledge and the other ghosts all the writing.

Agree on the split of income and expenses. Fifty percent is preferable even if one is better known as equal sharing ensures both parties act for their mutual benefit over the long-term.

Whose name goes first in the credits? Should this be alphabetical or will the one who is better known go first to ensure the project gets listed in those catalogues that use only one name and buyers have standing orders on all output under that name. Or a title like Dr may go first to ensure credibility.

The benefits of collaborating include twice the work done in half the time. The second person is an additional editor, so the quality of drafting is superior.

But the major benefit is in marketing. Each has their own networks, and each can speak for the other if interviews are needed. Their project is likely to reach more readers or viewers than you could on your own.

Learning on the job from the others' skills or field of knowledge is also a big benefit. Some claim that working on a book length project together is a more significant experience than a higher degree. It's an apprenticeship in creativity.

Other benefits include:

- Technology, e.g. how to transfer words and high resolution images between collaborators.
- Plotting on a video call where it's possible to retain conversations as a record of the process.
- Overcoming procrastination. A date with a partner gives a personal deadline. You feel obliged to write your share before you next meet.
- Varied workplaces can be more sociable. Some try the cappuccino approach of working in cafes, midway between workplaces. Of course if you work in another state or country, the coffees have to be virtual.
- Both can publicise the project or substitute for each other.

Non-fiction is often commissioned and co-authors may be put together for their expertise. Factual or educational writing is easier to co-author, as long as at least one of you has a logical mind.

Long fiction or a series require a different kind of emotional collaboration. Some adopt characters, or act out scenes to get the dialogue right or use mood music.

Being part of an anthology differs from co-writing because usually the editor commissions a specific article or story. That is, unless you are the editor/contributor, which means making thematic decisions about what goes in or needs rewriting.

Coping with criticism. You need a united front and with a co-writer it is wonderful to feel another is on your side. You can celebrate together too.

If co-writing is like marriage, when do you need to divorce?

- When one is doing an unfair share of the work.
- If one takes all the public credit.
- The external market changes or the project aims change.
- When you disagree more than you agree.
- It's not financially viable.

A sign of success is if you collaborate on another project.

> ## Authorpreneurial Hint
>
> Initiate a collaborative project. Sign a letter of agreement which is mutually acceptable.

Streamlining Research from Varied Sources

Decide who is your target audience.

Use their kind of language. For example, simplify technical terms for a non-computer orientated reader or music history for someone who knows nothing of classical composers. If you are writing for a child, use their level of vocabulary and simple sentences.

Check copyright if you are using any visuals such as maps, diagrams, photos or cartoons.

Get into the habit of recording where you found what, with dates and links, so you can check later or provide evidence, if editors, fact checkers or lawyers request it.

Acknowledge interviewees and/or send them copy to check. Keep their email address, phone and address (but not on the published article).

Create your own code (font/colour system) to distinguish what are quotes, and what are your observations or conclusions.

Name and date any recordings or disks. Keep them until after publication.

If there are two versions/interpretations/dates, cover yourself by phrases like: 'Opinions vary about ... A claims ..., but B suggests ... So it's difficult to verify this'.

Distinguish between 'primary sources' where you've interviewed or visited, and 'secondary' where you're repeating/reporting on what someone else said.

Controversial material needs to be written diplomatically. It is wise to use their exact words in quotation marks. Sometimes you don't need to draw a conclusion, let the reader do that.

Balance your material and be selective. Distinguish between the main facts, and any tiny unusual aspects found at the last minute. These could swamp the ordinary stuff you have read lots of times on the subject because it's novel to you.

If swamped in 'bits', construct a timeline of the person's life or the process. You may not write the final work in chronological order, but this helps order your thoughts.

Establish what is the overall conflict in what you've found in your research.

Is it the ideal versus reality or the public versus the private person? Alternatively is it the risk taker versus the need to compromise with bureaucracy/authority?

Consider whether interpretations of this person have been affected by either society's expectations for the times or the values of the writer-researcher. Might this include your own interpretation or that of others?

Tone. Is this objective reporting, propaganda for one side or an unusual angle? Are 'you' in there as 'I' the investigator (not recommended, unless it's the frustration of not finding out) or is it objective?

Have you provided a context? Decide if you need to explain for a non-expert what was happening then and how it differs from now. What is the most fascinating thing you've learnt? Start with that.

An anecdote is a mini-story that is relevant to the angle you are exploring. An example might be a subject who was a risk taker with a sense of humour. People remember anecdotes better than dates and although you can give them both it works best to start with the anecdote.

Questions

- Be clear about what you are trying to find out. This big question is a hypothesis. For example, was X's personal charm and appearance the major reason for achieving high office or was it other skills such as problem solving, delegation, and the ability to inspire in disastrous situations? Plus the ability to function on little sleep?
- Or, as a further example, is family modelling or school the greater influence in educational aspiration? Remember that your hypothesis may change during the project.

Compile 20 generic questions for interviewees. You also have the option to include them at the back of your book or article. It is important in terms of footnotes to learn the conventions, including author, page, and title for academic articles only, but keep bottom of the page or end notes in your final version to a minimum. Include only enough for the reader to follow up if especially interested. Don't plagiarise (pass off others' work as yours).

No research is wasted, but as a guide, any project is about 2/3 research and 1/3 writing. Don't get researchitus. You do not have to research forever. The skill of effective writing lies in what to select and what to leave out from your research. Set a time limit and maybe re-use the facts in another project.

Authorpreneurial Hint

Simplify your final version and cut it by 25%.

The Day to Day

Improving Work Style, Space and Image

How do you describe your occupation:

- When you are being interviewed?
- On official documents?
- On your business card?

How you describe yourself can sound egotistical or form a significant stage in others accepting what you do, and maybe offering work.

Is this your passion, part time occupation or full time work? Which aspect do you prefer and which do you ignore until overwhelmed? For example, doing tax, invoicing, business statements, filing, upgrading, originating and so on?

Find out how others see you.

Setting up a Work Space

- Invest in a comfortable, safe minimum work space, unless you are in the design business, then go for advertising your skills in your surrounds.
- Check you have insurance to cover visitors, portable electronic equipment etc.
- Have a separate entrance if you work from a home office.
- Tax deductions for work related expenses such as domestic costs e.g. cleaning.
- Teach your family perfect phone etiquette and manners for dealing with clients.
- Keep a reception space clear of clutter.
- Have a sample display area (also known as the brag wall), as the creative process intrigues visitors.

CV of a Creator

Unlike conventional Curriculum Vitae, an authorpreneur needs to indicate projects completed and the range of skills acquired by a creator who is self-employed in the business of ideas, even if not yet published or performed. Limit yourself to two pages (with visuals) or prepare it in a way that can be used in varied formats. Suggested headings include:

- Collaborative Projects
- Skills
- Publications
- Performances
- Work in Progress (WiP)
- Clients (if this is not confidential)
- Conferences and Workshops
- Exhibitions
- Qualifications/training
- Research Skills
- Residencies and Mentorships
- Awards
- Membership
- Translations/adaptations
- Reviews
- Lecturing/teaching
- Media coverage
- Referees
- Most unusual

Balance personal life with your work

A weekend may be mid-week for the self-employed. Work can become social, for example with interstate travel.

Are you becoming boring and only able to talk about your business?

- Is this phase temporary or permanent?
- Many artists change their content and write about another subject or learn about other fields and meet new people in this way.
- List aspects of your work style, which need improvement along with possible solutions.
- Can you afford to delegate or pay others?
- Simplify what you need others to help with.
- Or do you need blocks of time, to learn easier ways of 'maintaining' this yourself?

Do you have:

- A place for uninterrupted, concentrated work?
- Systems for finding crucial stuff in a hurry?
- Legal help with agreements?

- Colleagues who could substitute for you at short notice whose comparable standard of work you respect?
- Security, so work is not stolen.

Brand name:

- Is it your name on the business?
- What if you sell that business?
- If your business suddenly became astronomically successful, how would you cope?
- How might your reputation be destroyed? Any precautions in place?

The future:

- Any succession plan?
- If you were incapacitated, who would take over?
- Would your current records make sense to whoever inherits?
- Do you carry disability insurance?
- Have you got a will?
- Who holds the rights on certain properties?
- Any patents or trademarks?
- Do you have a literary executor?

Professionals:

Consider investing in an accountant, lawyer, tax agent, technical assistant or personal help. Judge which professional organisations offer the most relevant help for your work style.

> **Authorpreneurial Hint**
>
> Look at your working area as if you were a visitor or client. What impression does it give?

Mentoring

'Did you have a mentor?'
'Are you mentoring anyone?'
'What do you call the person being mentored?'

Some call them a 'mintie' but the proper term is a mentoree.

Mentoring is a highly paid 'corporate life coaching' trend, but many artists and writers have been voluntarily mentoring younger and less experienced practitioners for centuries.

Work role modelling is probably the closest definition because everybody mentors differently. Writing is a craft and the less experienced mentoree is like an apprentice who gains concentrated work experience with a master (or mistress) in self-employed creativity or the business of ideas.

Mentoring is not the same as coaching. It is not teaching nor tutoring and neither is it a sexual relationship. It is not a substitute parenting arrangement either. Most writers have parents although sometimes it is implied they don't.

Corporate mentoring where both participants are in a hierarchical business is very different because of the competitive aspect, whereas creators can have distinctive styles, and not be in direct competition for a job or promotion.

Generic life coaches are a bit like psychologists, whereas an author is likely to have specific job skills, such as crafting words, speaking, editing, marketing or researching that the newer mentoree may need to see in action.

Some organisations offer paid mentorships. The mentoree may pay or may be subsidised.

If you are looking for a mentorship consider:

- A practitioner with broad experience
- The ability to analyse and teach as well as do
- Availability

What does a mentor seek in a mentoree?

- Ideas
- Hard work

- Persistence and the ability to work towards long-term goals and relationship

Clarify ethical issues:
- Whether you are willing to act as a referee later
- Do not ask a mentoree to do unpaid work for the mentor's project
- Establish the degree of personal involvement
- Ensure confidentiality

What's in it for the mentor?

The pleasure of passing on skills and helping an enthusiastic creator to develop. Usually payment is not the motive as it is a mentors' market and many practitioners prefer to choose their own mentorees and not be bound by the 'administrivia' of bureaucracy that requires insurances and checks.

Modern mentoring is more likely to be electronic, via email or web chats and not limited by geography.

Ten mentoring hints

1. Have a trial session where either has the right to withdraw.

2. Exchange honest reasons for being involved.

3. Clarify whether the relationship is voluntary or payment is involved.

4. Agree on time limits for meetings, project and the length of the mentorship period. Be flexible but regular.

5. Plan a mixture of face to face, email, video or phone contacts. Snail mail is ok too.

6. Encourage some shadowing of the mentor's work style to find what is really involved.

7. Meet at the mentor's workplace to save mentor's time and provide easily accessible resources.

8. Accept that the mentoree's goals are likely to change as they become exposed to more opportunities.

9. Styles vary but criticism needs to be offered in a constructive manner.

10. Mentor should use the Socratic Method of asking strategic questions until the mentoree finds their own solution.

Niche Market: Mentoring Picture Books

Mistakenly, many assume picture books are an easy field to enter, so this is a good example of how to tackle a specialist niche which has a wide, international readership and often a long earning life, but which is technically challenging.

Long lasting picture books have indefinable 'flair' which breaks all the rules and a new readership, each six years, which is a generation. Any manuscript can be improved.

Ask why you are writing it? Be honest and ask yourself who your audience is. Is it a specific child or the child within you?

Overall, check it's an appropriate concept for the age group and has the potential for imaginative visuals. Is the text simplified and the logic established? Picture books or visual stories can be for all ages, including pre-teens, adolescents and adults. Some picture books are appropriate gifts for families because of their unique artwork or issues.

Concept: What is the story about? Is it a big enough concept for 32 pages? What is the underlying conflict, which provides the drama or tension?

Title: Consider the sound and length of the title. An ambiguous but brief or outrageously long title will attract this age group.

Limit the number of named characters or distinguish them quickly. For example, Zac and Zoe are too similar.

Logic of fantasy: Be consistent. Do adults 'know'?

Storyboard the text across a 32 page picture book, to indicate the variety of visuals for an art brief. Some pages may have very little text.

Is there any challenge for an illustrator? For example, do you have a unisex child character or non-human characters?

Decide whether you want print, eBook or audio formats, or all of these. Will you use photographs, collage or a cartoon style?

How many words should you have? There are no set rules but under 200 words is a guide. Some have none as picture books without text can be very emotionally involving.

Get the text right first. Don't organise an illustrator who is family or friend, as often the publisher prefers to commission illustrations.

Some creators are illustrator-authors. They are privileged to think in words and visuals.

In general, use the present tense as it is shorter and more immediate.

Concepts should be presented in a child's level of vocabulary, not an adult's. For example, write 'You're good at making things', rather than 'you are inventive' unless the term 'inventor' is central to the story.

The basic rule is show, don't tell. Rather than say the character is inventive, give three outrageous examples of what she's made that convey this such as an upside down pet-feeder, goggles for onion chopping without crying and ...?

Dated clichés like 'pleased as punch' convey little to this age group. Use specifics such as 'On Friday', rather than 'One day'. It is great to include noisy words, but make them easy to read.

Check the logic of your writing. Don't have 'flew through the door'. It would be a doorway. Also a fantasy needs to have an internal logic.

Make every verb count – use spluttered rather than moved, for example. Then see how many words you can take out.

Is a picture book the most appropriate format for this concept? Maybe it is an illustrated story or an animation or script?

Will the story translate into other cultures and other mediums? Aim for page turning quality.

Enjoy the process.

Authorpreneurial Hint

Pitch an animation/film/merchandising project based on your picture book concept.

Fans, Reviews, Critics and Privacy

Fame sounds attractive, if you don't have it. If your controversial project is likely to attract attention, you may attract critics but also some 'nutters' whose interpretation of your work may differ from your intention. Decide before media interviews, how much personal stuff you're prepared to reveal. Does it include family names, addresses, personal anecdotes etc.

Unless fiction is based on particular issues or wins awards, it generates little publicity. But colleagues will be aware and contribute to your reputation based on the quality of your work. This leads to further work offers, or not!

Often a book or character or product may be known but not the author or designer. Some creators prefer this.

It's a fine line between being accessible for genuine fans or being annoyed by persistent callers. Some writers have public and private numbers or pages. Calls can be screened via voice mail.

'Stalkers' can 'tag' their comments with your name, so you are attributed with opinions you didn't utter, or they can suggest you are closely involved, when you are not. This can be hard to remove.

If you've written an autobiography or family history, you're guaranteed to annoy a relative. Clarify that this book is your researched version and they can write their own.

Don't relax too much during enjoyable radio interviews with attentive interviewers. 'Off the record' is not always respected. Or you may inadvertently reveal material, which is permanently recorded, or podcast for new audiences.

Ensure your 'autograph' is distinctive from your credit card signature. Creators can't afford to lose their hard won money to scams.

If you publicise dates and times where you'll be working interstate or internationally, hint there is someone at home. Otherwise you're giving a burglar a useful timetable.

Fan mail can be poignant, heartwarming and/or sustaining. Occasionally it reflects that fiction imitates life, as readers assume you are writing about them. 'You Wrote About Me!' Was this unintentional, a mistake, an error of fact or just a compliment, because you evoked a credible character? Legal advice may be needed in extreme cases.

The etiquette for reviews is that you don't challenge a bad one (or a good one!) unless there is an error of fact not opinion. But you may raise a general issue for discussion, indirectly related to that subject.

Fan mail belongs to its writer, not the recipient. So if you wish to display fan mail in an exhibition, you need permission.

Date and minute any unpleasant incidents related to your book, as obsessives can consume your working time, requiring paperwork, which you may have to find, to prove your legitimate claim.

Collectors or archivists may want your work, even the drafts.

Celebrate any 'firsts' like finishing the manuscript, a contract, an advance, publication or even your first fan letter.

Memorabilia include collectables from the research, or publicity relating to the book. Now much is electronic, some writers collect their draft print version(s) as well as two copies of each book edition (well wrapped) so it doesn't fade.

Consider a clippings album and decide whether to make it chronological or per project. This can be useful for later quotes from reviews on new editions or as support for multi-media adaptation proposals.

Privacy can be an issue: obsessives may quote you out of context or use a tiny section of your writing.

The speed of social media may mean 'fame' for five minutes, but weird comments added cannot always be removed easily under online entries.

To avoid being overwhelmed, some popular authors have 'generic' Q and A on their websites or a sheet to send. Others, especially children's book creators often respond individually to child fans (unless 30 the same arrive from a class assignment).

Authorpreneurial Hint

Be wary of forwarding emails; remember they may be private or contain controversial information beneath.

Talkback Radio, from an Author's Perspective

If the radio station is to ring you at home, turn off noisy appliances nearby. Inevitably the fridge has a heart attack, the dishwasher cycle goes into super noise rinse or the neighbour mows their grass. Or someone knocks at the door (pin up a note or leave the door unlocked).

Turn off your mobile, unless it has to be available as a backup phone for them to contact you initially. Remember to keep the phones apart or they interfere electronically with each other.

A radio interview can be done in the studio, on your landline or even on a mobile. The station prefers to have you in the studio to control the sound quality, but that may add considerable travelling time for you. However, for a talkback, that may be essential to control the multiple lines for callers.

Make sure you negotiate the location, especially if it is peak hour or the middle of the night.

The 'Tardis' is the term used to describe a tiny studio, where you are linked with an interstate presenter or producer. Effectively it means you are talking to yourself or a blank wall. It helps to imagine a face and talk to it.

A talkback is different from a 'straight' interview in that you'll be required to answer questions as 'an expert' or at least comment on callers' points.

Jot names of callers on a pad, so you can use the right name. Or add their query, in case you get off the topic.

The person who calls you first will be the producer, but you'll be talking to the presenter next. Don't use the wrong name. Usually the producer is an excellent psychologist who diplomatically says what a wonderful subject or how well you answered, or that they don't usually get even two callers in this time slot!

Check on the exact times and whether they are in the same time zone as you. A co-author in Wellington, New Zealand is two hours ahead of Melbourne, so when doing an ABC dual talkback interview, participants need to know whose time zone they are in.

Don't under-estimate the audience of middle of the night programs. It's not just insomniacs who ring in. Often podcasts are made, and listened to, much later. They can also be Googled by subject tags. For example an ABC overnight talkback (at 3.30am Melbourne time) on family history collected many listeners keen to write their stories. That was national and the podcast was around for Googling. (Luckily the studio calls you 15 minutes beforehand to check you're awake or that your alarm worked.)

Jot down four to five points you wish to make about the topic, or useful links that can go on the station website later.

Answer the question and talk about the subject, don't just 'plug' your book. Your aim is to provide an enjoyable conversation on air.

Listen to the recording afterwards, and decide on ways to improve next time. For example, if you were nervous, slow down and lower your voice to sound more authoritative. Don't be afraid to use anecdotes (mini-stories) about yourself.

Luckily it doesn't matter what you wear on radio, but next time it might be a web-cam. Or TV camera.

What happens if no one calls in? You just keep chatting about the subject. What happens if someone you know rings in, and admits on air they are your ex-boyfriend etc. Relax. The producer has a control button with a time lag of several seconds.

It is useful to have a humorous, short piece with which to end.

Remember any noise is magnified. If you have notes, take out the clips, spread the pages out beforehand, and don't make turning noises.

Have a glass of water nearby in case your throat tickles.

If the interview ends suddenly for a commercial break or the news, you might be cut off, and left wondering if you should stay on the phone. Just hang up. They won't necessarily ring you back to say what a terrific job you did.

Enjoy yourself. Remember that for every response there were 100 listeners – as you'll discover in subsequent months.

Authorpreneurial Hint

Listen to podcast segments of the program on which you are to appear to analyse the style.

TV Interviews from an Author's Perspective

Are you flattered or fearful that you're to be interviewed on television? As a visual medium, TV travels far and fast, but use the few minutes effectively. Prepare one major point, but in anecdotal (story) or quotable one liners.

Are you to be interviewed on community, state or national broadcasting? Is it live to air or pre-recorded and can other channels pick it up? Will there be any opportunity to edit? Check if your book cover can be scanned in a separate shot.

Look at the opportunity from the viewpoint of the producer or the audience. What do they want from you? They don't want a spiel about how good your book is. They want facts, entertainment or vicarious (secondhand) experience as you share with them how you researched this subject. A sense of humour or even wit is appreciated and may mean a return visit.

How should you look? Solid colours work better and avoid distractors like dangling earrings or striped shirts.

The station prefers to have you in the studio to control quality. Some programs just insert a clip filmed elsewhere.

Watch the program afterwards; not for ego, but for ways you can improve. For instance don't waggle your head or close your eyes so much. TV takes more time than radio with makeup and hair etc. but often is more widely received, especially if it is news.

It is preferable to be controversial but you don't want to be quoted out of context. Remember that you'll be edited, so practise saying 30 second grabs.

Have something colourful to 'show'. Are you being interviewed 'in character' dressed as your own character? Or as the author?

Makeup and hair may be done but occasionally you may be shot 'natural' so comb your hair beforehand.

Are you on commercial TV or ABC? It's important to avoid making an advertorial, but you can use the book title.

Ask for a copy of your segment, or permission to have a link from your website as it is useful to have movie clips.

What impression do you wish to give? Do you want to appear authoritative and know what you're talking about, or memorable and witty? The important thing is to get the 'idea' content across perhaps by using logic or humour.

The Green Room isn't always green. This is the waiting room where food and drink are available prior to your slot. You may meet 'celebs' or interesting egos there but don't be put off by their attitudes. Everyone shows nerves in different ways.

Will you need to relate to a puppet or costumed 'creature' who is non-human, on camera? If so, just shake any appendage as if it were a hand and respond to the face.

If you are doing a cooking program or a 'how to' it's essential to prepare a finished item as well as the stages.

Although your TV appearance may be unrelated to your book, e.g. if you are a quiz contestant, the audience will be reminded of your author role, indirectly.

Scams, scandals and protests are what they will remember, but not the details. So your reputation may be affected.

If the TV appearance is really bad, don't use it, but you can mention you've been on So and So's program in your CV. Unless you prefer a selective memory lapse.

Prepare by practising on a web-cam with your own questions.

> **Authorpreneurial Hint**
>
> Get a colourful prop to show or use in photographs and on camera.

The Etiquette of Book Launches and Literary Events

These hints were part of a launch talk for a book on etiquette, but also apply to anthologies, which attract potential buyers associated with all the contributors.

If you attend a launch:

- Buy a book. No such thing as a free launch.
- Get it autographed and dated (worth 1000% more later, maybe).
- Don't ask the author for a free copy unless you are a reviewer for a mainstream outlet with millions of readers.

- If you are in a relationship with the author, be prepared to be part of a rent a crowd if no one else fronts.

If you agree to launch it:

- Read the whole book, preferably before you say 'Yes, I'll launch it' because there could be some words you prefer not to say in public (especially if it has an X rated section).
- Make sure you have some sticky markers in your launch copy, and read quick extracts with page references, so the author knows you've read it.
- Don't talk all the time about your book, which isn't being launched today, even if you think it is a much better book of the same kind.
- Keep it short. One minute per contributor is the going boredom rate, even for an anthology.
- Ensure you can pronounce the title, and author's name, and publisher even before you've had a drink.
- Avoid microphone wobble and don't ask, 'Can you hear me at the back?'
- Don't break the champagne over the book, it isn't a ship.

If it's your book being launched:

- Write a book with lots of contributors who have many friends and millions of relatives, especially mums with cash.
- Choose a location others wish to visit and where they can find parking, even in peak hour.
- Get the foreword written by someone willing to bring/attract others to the launch.
- Place a quirky promo in the media a week before, drawing attention to the title.
- Have a visual gimmick that is likely to attract media photographers.
- Promote the launch to those who might be interested in the content but for whom a launch is a novelty (not literary editors who yawn at another launch invite).
- Provide a map, with coordinates for the geographically challenged.
- Bookshops are great because they have their own cash registers, and the book will continue to be sold after you leave. And their posters are read by people who read by choice.
- Have a media release ready with time, place, price, ISBN (librarians order from this) and some attention getter, to use before, during and after launch.

- Invite a launcher who will attract those who have enough cash to buy books e.g. not impoverished students with debts.
- Check there's a change float, a credit machine and a receipt book and someone apart from the author to handle the money. The author will (hopefully) be busy signing.
- Take digital photos to send with captions to local media immediately.
- Get someone to take a photo of the book cover with the authors.
- Unless it's totally egotistical or boring, get a copy of the launcher's talk to use as part of your article about the book launch.
- Write up the launch complete with ISBN, price and where the book is now available.
- Don't gush too much about all those who helped you … your dog or pet croc doesn't need a credit.

Autographing Etiquette

- Have a pen which works and doesn't smudge.
- If no one wants to buy a book, look busy with your rent a crowd.
- Only sign after the reader has paid for the book (sit on the other side of the cash register.
- Check on the exact spelling of the buyer's name or whose name they want written. For 'me' needs clarification.
- Whoever spills the red wine on the book pays but coffee is a 50/50 split.
- Sign on the title page which has the author name.
- With multiple authors, agree to all sign on the title page, or alongside their name on the table of contents not on the individual story.
- Offer to autograph any remaining copies so they can be displayed later near the cash register with an 'autographed' sticker.

Etiquette of Literary Events

E   for Etiquette.

T   for Time management. Keep all talks brief!

I   I-itus Don't talk about yourself all the time. And don't read unless the extracts are humorous and under a minute.

Q   Quit talking when the first one leaves.

U   Understanding that if it's your first publication, you're allowed to gush a little (or your mum is).

E   Evaluate, and send thank yous.

T Thematic food or dress gives launch goers something to talk about. You can even scan your book cover onto a cake top.

T Ties and required 'dress'. Remember that single colour clothes photograph better and earrings sway distractingly on TV news.

E Exit. Always have pamphlets available with website links.

> **Authorpreneurial Hint**
>
> If the book hasn't arrived in time for the launch, display the cover and take pre-paid orders. Have a small gift for the launcher, not just the autographed book.

Adaptations, Translations and Judging

Adaptations

If a producer invests in adapting from book into film, theatre, animation or television, considerations include:

- Proven popularity and recognition of the character or book
- A good story
- Media worthiness of creator
- Topical issues which can be linked such as environmental
- Availability of rights
- Potential funding/investment
- Location
- Cast size
- Attractiveness for international sales
- Option fee and budget
- Support in kind
- Bankability/reputations of those who might be cast

Suggestion: Prepare a one page brief of the adaptation strengths of your work including such items as the range of settings, number of characters etc.

Translations

To see the cover of your familiar work translated into a language you can't read is a thrill.

- Keep two copies of each for your records.
- Translation rights are sold by agent or publisher at annual international book fairs (such as Frankfurt, London or New York) or in the long follow-up period. They are listed under subsidiary rights in contracts and the split may vary between publishers.
- Occasionally these translations may be available only within that country e.g. China, or in a format read only by locals, which may differ from the version read in other countries or international schools where that language is taught. For example, sandwich is unknown in French, for lunch. Le Sandwich Americain is different.
- Colloquial: Chinglish (Chinese English), Australian, American and Indian are some versions of English. And it's not always about 'mum' to 'mom' or 'tap' to 'faucet'.
- The costs of translation will be covered by the local publisher and there will often be a new cover to suit that market. For example, a photograph rather than an illustration. The author may have approval rights and if the translation occurs after the film, the book cover is likely to be film linked.
- Informal translations occur with favourite children's books, especially if they are used with dual languages in literacy programs or web chats. But if they are widely used on whiteboards in classrooms, permission fees must be paid.
- Proof reading is a challenge. Get a native speaker to check the manuscript. Sometimes 'parental hints for reading' are included with Chinese picture book translations, plus other additions you need to know about.
- Translations into Braille and Auslan signing for the deaf are usually permitted by the author for no fee.
- Censorship: You may be asked to approve or change material for the local market. This may relate to 'swearing' or to ethical issues linked to race or religion. This is up to you!
- Speaking at a conference or accepting an invitation to speak in the country may assist translation offers and book sales. But there's often a year's time lag. Books may not be available in time for your first visit, even if printed in that country.
- Customs regulations may halt imports of your books or add extra taxes and duty. Much depends upon whether they are labeled 'commercial' or samples for study or gifts.

- Certain types of books 'travel' well into other cultures, but humour is often local, and doesn't translate well. Picture books are faster to translate and the visuals help in another culture.

Judging and Awards

Winning an international award increases interest in translation. Especially if a gold medal sticker is on the cover. Just as a reviewer performs a 'sifting' service for time poor readers, indicating why a book is worth reading, so a judge should indicate the basis on which an award is made.

Here is one judge's criteria for fiction: The test of a good story is if it stays with you, and if it reads well aloud.

Some considerations when choosing winners are:

- Structure or choreographing of the idea
- Easily distinguishable characters
- Underlying conflict to provide the drama
- Evoking setting, both time and place
- Subtlety, so the writer hints rather than repeats
- Humour
- Subtext
- Twist
- Credible dialogue which advances the plot
- Relevant title as first clue
- Compassionate portrayal showing strengths and weaknesses
- Flair, the indefinable quality

The criteria for non-fiction are very similar but must include recognition of facts researched. If you are judging, what do you consider to be the most important criteria? Not your personal relationship to the creator of the book!

Re-Jacketing or Re-titling?

A re-issue of your work, via adaptation or translation or even a new edition offers the rare opportunity of 'tweaking.'

For example, the original cover may not have indicated the type of book. It might have looked 'girly' or 'bloke-ish' and alienated some potential readers. Perhaps you need to have adventurous male and female characters on the cover to indicate the story more accurately.

Often 're-jacketing' decisions are made by the marketing department rather than the author, but you can make suggestions. A new title may be better suited for the community of the translation, as culturally some words or even names may be offensive or derogatory. Certain colours or numbers are considered lucky in Asian cultures.

Looking at your work from another perspective can lead to re-working and better quality in the final version.

- What were the weaknesses/strengths of your original title/cover?
- Justify the cost of a new cover or title.

> ### Authorpreneurial Hint
>
> Justify why an investor should provide a million in your currency to develop your concept in a different medium.

Surviving Rejection

Separate the personal from the work: If you are a beginning writer, not being accepted for immediate publication is the first rejection. That's the hardest. Creators of heavily autobiographical works, often take rejection of their titles personally as if their lives are valued at nothing. Separating the feeling of being personally rejected from the work not being accepted takes practice.

Odds: There are 57 varieties of rejection, including a bad review, criticism or being overlooked. Not being read is another kind of rejection. Pragmatic reasons for rejection include the small market, writing on speculation and the odds of getting out of the slush pile being a gamble of 1:1000.

Emotional Insurance: Recognise that rejection is the norm. Knock backs for reasons of length, tone, style, subject matter, timing or just no reason can all wound. Creators need emotional insurance and that includes diversifying. Writing more or recycling is also a form of emotional insurance that can defuse the wounding impact of ideas being ignored. Doing some market research about prospective readers and 'tweaking' the project to suit, will also reduce rejection.

Status Quo: Creators tend to feel rejected. One reason is the size of the gap between the personal aspiration and the public reality. All writers know they are Nobel Prize quality, in their heads; it is just the transition to page or screen which creates the gap. And not all judges have 20:20 vision.

Timing: Not all readers respond immediately when a creator has offered their work to public exposure. There is often a considerable time lag. The topic may also be ahead of its time or there have been too many others recently published on the same subject. Or if submitted to a publisher, pre-Christmas is when they clear their desks and in-trays, regardless.

Being overlooked is probably rejection with a longer impact. 'I've been long listed, instead of short listed' is a witty response.

New Direction: Being left out, left off or ignored energises some creators into starting afresh and creating a better project.

Reviews: A bad or inaccurate review affects most creators. Except the writers who claim not to read them. A few negative comments can niggle because there is some truth to them; others are so outrageous that laughter is the best remedy.

Criticism: Use it to evaluate. If the points were valid they can be useful in a rewrite. Ask yourself, what was the motive of the reviewer?

Were they objective or subjective? Did they give critical reasons and examples which indicate thoughtful evaluation and thorough reading? Or is it revenge in a small market, by a potential competitor? Is the criticism based on the work the reviewer thought you should have written or is it a pet peeve of the reviewer regardless of your subject?

How to Deal With a Bad Review

Off you go to the naughty corner until you learn how to say something nice about me.

How to respond to unfounded criticism: One possible response is to write an article about the ethics of reviewing and offer it to the parent publication as an indirect reply to an ignorant critic of others' work. Being rejected for the ideas content or the way it was written is a different matter. You need to assess the quality of your writing or the scope of possible unusual ideas.

Feeling artistically overlooked when some significant literary short list is announced is a common reaction. Taking it personally and complaining about judges' ignorance or bias, or 'putting down' competitors is futile and self-destructive. Even if you have 'pulled' a project for moral reasons.

Awards: Although it is useful for authors to be 'listed' or award winners, ultimately commercial sales and a loyal readership count more. The dilemma is that the size of the marketing budget determines how well a book or author is promoted and that is often linked to award listings and whether titles are even entered. It can be expensive to enter six copies for every contest and some publishers decide the book isn't worth the risk.

Rejection Quote of the Year contest? For example, years ago, the manuscript for a humorous non-fiction book about domestic time management was rejected by Paul Hamlyn Publishers with the comment 'We don't publish fiction.' Subsequently it was published elsewhere and did well as *Houseworking; The Unsuperperson's Guide to Sharing the Load.*

Check out places that are supportive to writers such as the ASA and the Society of Children's Book Writers and Illustrators (SCWBI) or form your own support group to share rejections and 'toast' acceptances. It is always helpful to share with a small group of peers.

List ten possible markets, and work your way through them. One persistent writer cracked it on the 39th try, went into reprints and earned a reasonable return from subsidiary rights across ten years.

If necessary change direction – take a detour to a new project to feel enthused or use humour and rejection slips for wallpaper as a design statement in your office. Alternatively you might write a humorous article on rejection.

Writers in for the permanent work style of self-employed freelancer have to develop ways of sustaining themselves such as:

- Diversifying, and having emotional investment in other projects at different stages.

- Recycling that rejected project in another format or to another prospective market.
- Re-read and maybe re-write to higher quality or a different audience.
- Reassure yourself that the project is high quality but maybe political, timely or economic reasons stopped it.
- Rationalise that one in ten projects get up.
- 'Cannibalise' parts of the rejected project for re-use.

> ## Authorpreneurial Hint
>
> Read about famous author rejections to comfort yourself.

Health Warnings for Authors

- Never write 'too close to home' or family and friends may be upset, disown or sue you.
- Keep your author photo within five years of your real face and shape.
- Murphy's Law – the cost of bank exchange fees to convert from foreign sales may exceed your income from obscure currencies with lots of zeros.
- Readers often assume fiction is autobiography, especially the sexual parts.
- Ex-lovers consider their love life private.
- A 'thesis' does not a book make.
- Beware of pirates of the on-line intellectual property kind. IP can also mean International Piracy.
- 'Prolific' is a put down.
- If you use a pseudonym, remember it.
- Back up! Your computer will crash on deadline and the technician will earn more in 15 minutes than your entire royalty period.
- Be wary of flattery! What have you written? Anything I might have read? Are you famous? Or, I loved your book. I got it for 10 cents from the op-shop.
- If introduced as a 'real live author' consider the alternative.
- Retirement is not an option.

Despite these warnings, the creative health of most authors is enriched by the imaginative satisfaction of their work.

> ## Authorpreneurial Hint
>
> Write your own ten satirical hints relevant to your subject, for use in concluding talks.

4: Case Studies

Charitable Projects, Innovations and Contracting Payment

Educational factual writing is often commissioned to fit a series and initiated by a publisher. Sometimes there's a collaboration proposed between a health or safety organisation or a charity who wish to get an issue discussed in the school or parental community and a publisher and/or writers.

Often the finances are problematic with 'worthy' organisations who wish books to be written on their subject, but who are naïve about the research/writing time and skills required and how best to finance and distribute the project.

A fee for service is common with the copyright held by the organisation. Unfortunately, so is no money for writers, despite many meetings and drafts. This might be common but it is not acceptable.

Maybe you feel mean about billing a 'charity' or worthy project whose philosophy you support. But you will work more effectively for them if you are not feeling frustrated at non-payment or feeling 'taken for granted' as a writer. Alternatively, regard this as your 'soul' project and expect to work as a volunteer.

Administrators or experts are salaried, and you are self-employed.

A one hour 'freebie' meeting on your part may be a half day commitment for no fee.

If the 'host' needs to apply for funding or 'in kind' support which is dependent upon your writing a detailed proposal and costings, decide on your time limit. Consider adapting a former proposal or use a generic response.

If the process is innovative and the content interests you, plus you enjoy meeting these colleagues, regard the project as educational for you, and waive payment.

However, you need to limit the number of 'freebie' meetings requiring peak hour travel and/or preparation of briefs or proposals unless there is some likelihood of return.

Often these projects are dropped anyway. Writing by committee where each 'expert' wants a re-write, creates endless work and dilutes the original purpose.

Or it may be a project which later attracts favourable publicity by association leading to further work.

Clarify who holds copyright as this affects later payments like PLR and ELR and any subsidiary rights negotiations.

Educational Collaboration: Magabooks

This authorpreneurial case study is relevant because of the innovative magabook format and shared royalty contract with a packaging publisher initiated by writers and shared with a hospital.

Eventually the hospital benefitted financially and in terms of publicity for the health issues, as did the patients' families and the books were sold into an international publisher's distribution. Co-writers retained part royalties.

Magabooks are a new visual concept for educational books. 'Mag' refers to magazine. 'Book' relates to book. So these publications are highly visual, almost comic in style, but not Manga as in Japanese comic visuals.

Aimed at the visually literate, the graphic designer has a major input. However, it was important to ensure that the intellectual content, such as health and medical facts, were also conveyed to the target audience. Initially co-authors were approached with other creators (dramatists, illustrators, publishers and actors) by Melbourne's Royal Children's Hospital 'Murdoch Institute', who specialise in research on children's illnesses.

The hospital was concerned that young patients were having a hard time as often their classmates did not understand the demands of certain illnesses such as epilepsy or diabetes, and neither did some parents. Educational authorities also needed to know when certain absences from school were legitimate, and how to accommodate individual health needs.

Over afternoon tea, obesity, risk taking, genes, height, epilepsy, diabetes and children born with indeterminate gender were discussed. A fast medical overview with visuals was given.

The brief was to find 'artistic' ways of getting health messages across to primary and secondary students as well as to the parents and communities in which these children live. Both doctors and self-employed freelancers were busy people, and didn't have time to waste unless the briefs could be shaped into realistic aims. There were long discussions on various ways to get the message across, especially to teenagers.

Proposals were requested on health research areas and the best methods of conveying these educationally. In the end magabooks became the choice of medium. Unless the content was related to the curriculum, teachers wouldn't use it and it was here that educational packagers/publishers were approached as they had extensive curriculum experience and could see the commercial possibilities of linking hospital requirements with educational needs.

Safety and health tend to be viewed by students as boring, so both layout and content needed a mixture of 'faction' and formats such as Q and A, diary entries, 'active' menus and activities. Coming up with the initial concept areas was difficult and catchy titles were vital as it was obviously off-putting to call a booklet 'obesity'.

Agreement was reached on 24 topics which would fit under curriculum headings. The Murdoch Institute medical specialists provided data, especially of the lesser known medical areas. They also checked what co-authors wrote and suggested any necessary alterations. It was difficult to turn a complex medical problem into one liners using simple vocabulary. However the job was to make obscure medical conditions accessible.

On average, 10-20 re-writes were needed on most pages. It was also necessary to conceptualise graphics and access stock photo sites. Later the publishers would pay for the most appropriate. 'Hi-resolution' transfers soon became a problem as some photos were super 'hi-res' and clogged emails. When this happened drop boxes were used although keeping track of so much information was hard.

As intended, the material is informative and factual and the designs and illustrations are exciting and innovative. Together with the Murdoch

Institute the co-authors hope these serve their purpose in bringing greater 'health and understanding' to both children and adults.

IP Rights

With an intellectual property such as a picture book, there is the issue of who controls which rights, in which territories and formats (related to text or visuals) when the author and illustrator are not the same creator. The publisher may control subsidiary rights, but with the speed of change, some of these may not be specified in the original contract of a long-term seller. With multi-media, many contributors may be involved and the issue of payment or a delayed share in profits or skills in kind, gets complicated.

It is essential to clarify your rights and limit terms before you move into new projects.

Long life best seller in varied media: Cake Eating Rooftop Hippo

Picture book *There's a Hippopotamus on Our Roof Eating Cake*, first published in 1980 by Hodder and illustrated by Deborah Niland and constantly in print, is now a series of seven. Translated into Chinese, Braille, a 16 minute film by Pocket Bonfire, it has been screened internationally and the story is frequently read on children's TV programs like ABC Play School and Yamba's Playtime for Indigenous literacy. Garry Ginivan's theatrical production toured nationally as Hippo! Hippo! It is now published by Penguin.

Why the long life? Reasons include:

- Willingness to experiment with new media opportunities.
- An original story with a theme of friendly reassurance.
- Simple, child-appealing illustrations.
- Subject themes: The picture books cover issues about which children may be apprehensive, so although not 'therapy' they tend to be re-read when there's a new baby, starting school, going to hospital, on holidays or when there is a birthday.
- Educational link via classroom play scripts and parental market.
- Resources available on author website.
- A generation is about six years, then there's another readership.

A well loved book or character belongs to the reader/audience, rather than just to the creator and it's important to retain the concept's reputation.

The speed and intensity of cross media reactions to the removal of the word 'smack' from the Penguin edition indicates the challenges. Sometimes words travel further and faster than their creators.

Censorship and Imaginative Ownership: Hippo 'smack'

Abridged version of article first published in *The Looking Glass: new perspectives on children's literature,* vol. 12 no. 2, 2008, available at www. the-looking-glass.net

Censorship or the Curious, Electronic eFair of the Hippo 'smack'?

Background: Originally published by Hodder, the 'Hippo' titles were moved to Penguin for distribution reasons in 2004. When a 25th anniversary reprint was planned, a line in the first title was queried. At a point in the story where the little girl gets in trouble for drawing on Daddy's best book, it was suggested that the original 'Daddy gave me a smack' be changed to 'Daddy growled at me'.

Being the creator of a well known book like *There's a Hippopotamus on Our Roof Eating Cake* has been a quiet pleasure for over a quarter of a century since the original 1980 publication. However, in November 2004 when consideration of the 'smack' became an issue of contemporary family values in the new Penguin edition, authorship became a media responsibility.

The sequence is significant as it is a case of cross media coverage in a time of rapid electronic transfer on an issue which escalated into a volatile discussion of censorship. From email, to web chats, mobile messages, radio and TV interviews and 'experts' being interviewed and even becoming an issues clear thinking piece for school students in The Age's Education Section, the use of the electronic medium, in McLuhan-ish terms, affected the message. That is why I have used the term 'eFair'.

It is important to state there never was conflict between author and publisher, as the original editorial change from 'smack' to 'growled' had been agreed, a week prior and the author-publisher relationship was extremely amicable. After listening to Penguin's reasons, I had reluctantly agreed despite believing stories should be read in the cultural context in which they were written. However in some interviews, the subsequent media coverage implied publisher censorship. This was not so.

My view that, once it is published, a book belongs to the imagination of the reader, not the author, was confirmed by the issue of the 'smack'. Readers claimed definite ownership of this book, especially parents for whom it was their favourite book during their childhood. And beyond the book, it is the positive or negative emotions associated with childhood which are so passionate, and which this book symbolises in the reassuring role of an imaginary friend.

The majority who contacted me with passionate views were young fathers who wanted to read it to their children in its original version. Whether the wording was changed or not, they wanted the opportunity to use the book as a focus of family discussion. So many dads wanting to read to their kids was a plus!

A second group were the 'twenty-something' producers, presenters and journalists who had fond memories of the book or older media colleagues who had read it to their children. So the issue became topical because of media opinion choosers.

Political topicality was a factor too. The 'hippo smack' editing incident occurred while various politicians were adopting children's reading as a 'worthy' vote catcher and because changing a phrase in a book was tenuously linked to censorship.

Media-wise, this 'hippo smack' incident is significant because it became a 'news' rather than a 'feature' issue. It also crisscrossed the local cultural gap between the ABC/The Age 'serious' media and the more tabloid, talkback Herald Sun, Channel 7 and 9 commercial audiences, as well as regional radio and television. But the fastest spread was via the Internet.

The original issue of the changing of a phrase in a new edition of a picture book was 'lifted' electronically into web chats where extracts from considered articles were quoted in and out of context. Sometimes the online web chatters had not seen the book, but felt that they had licence to comment because 'childhood' is valued. They felt they were experts because they had been children, have children or knew what is right for children.

Adult readers projected their feelings about how parents had disciplined them onto the proposed change in the book, so a few views were extreme and cannot be quoted here. Cynics commented that it was a very successful PR exercise by the author. But since the book was not available until scheduled reprinting four months later, it would have been a pointless PR exercise when no copies were available for sale.

So, here is a summary of how this curious, electronic eFair unfolded.

Although letters to the editor are in the public domain and can be used, ironically in checking with the Arts Law Centre of Australia service I discovered that legally I do not own the emails addressed to me as the author of the book and that I have to get permission to quote in full. This is difficult, as many were hotmail or had no return eDresses or bounced. However, I am legally entitled to summarise the major points even if not using the names. So I have.

November 3rd 2004

There had been a news item on ABC radio about the UK Parliament being pressured by the child protection lobby to pass a law banning smacking. So, I wrote to The Age about it:

> Letter to the Editor: Smacking
>
> The child protection lobby wants smacking of children to be banned by parliamentary law. As the author of the 25-year-old children's classic *There's a Hippopotamus on Our Roof Eating Cake* I've been asked to remove the 'Daddy gave me a smack' in the next Penguin edition and replace it with 'Daddy growled at me'. While I do not support child abuse, I do not want to change the text because many of the million child readers know the book word for word, but I will probably bow to political pressure. What do readers think?
>
> Hazel Edwards

This provoked immediate responses for interviews and a flood of emails and phone calls from readers and talkback radio, who favoured for a variety of reasons retaining the original wording by about nine to one.

Later that day, Macquarie Network radio pre-recorded an interview and followed with talkback radio (this was repeated several times and other media outlets started to chase the story) which provoked readers' letters to the editor.

November 4th 2004

The Age education editor's feature article 'Editing Smacks of Censorship' was particularly important because it was syndicated around the country to The Sydney Morning Herald and the West Australian as well as being online immediately, enabling segments to be electronically copied or quoted. Likewise, the Melbourne Herald Sun photographic story was available online as well as in print.

On the morning of November 4th, the phone started ringing at 7am, and as I stood dripping, I was glad it was not a web cam.

'We're fifteen minutes away.'

'Away from what?'

'Your house. Please don't let the other channel speak to you first.' The producers and interviewers from Channel 7's Today Tonight and Channel 9's A Current Affair news commentary programs vied for 'different' angles, and agreed between themselves not to be on the premises at the same time.

On request, I changed my top for each TV segment so the colour was different. In between the phone rang constantly until one of the crew took it off the hook, despite phone radio interviews and talkback with most interstate morning and evening programs. In between I tried to keep in contact with Penguin's publicist and later heard that, after visiting me, the current affairs television crew had gone unannounced to Penguin Books to interview the publisher and that they had also received many emails.

As a family, we tried to watch the simultaneous current affairs TV programs and were surprised at how little was used after the two to three hours spent and also at the editorial attempts to suggest conflict.

Channel 7 Today Tonight: November 4th 2004

Note: Transcripts of introductions to television current affairs programs are available online and these often follow the pattern of stressing a dilemma.

- As the political correctness court cases fly, another controversy rages over a book called There's a Hippopotamus on Our Roof Eating Cake.
- One line in particular has come under fire. The central character is reprimanded with the line 'Daddy gave me a smack' and the book's publishers, Penguin, want this changed to the less contentious 'Daddy growled at me.'
- Author, Hazel Edwards says she would prefer the line stays in her re-released book.
- 'I think it is comparable to taking out cultural references when you translate a book from other cultures,' Ms Edwards said. 'And I think it's important for our children to see stories from our past and also read about other cultures and see them in context.'

- Penguin publisher, Laura Harris says the changes reflect the attitudes of today, rather than those of 25 years ago when the book was first written. 'We felt by changing that line we perhaps gave a message where children can decide which disciplinary actions they want to take – that smacking wasn't the only way of disciplining a child,' Ms Harris said. 'The fact is smacking is not an everyday choice as it was in 1979.'
- Joe Tucci from Australians Against Child Abuse applauds the move. 'I think Penguin have shown a lot of foresight to actually encourage the author to review the book,' Mr Tucci said. 'And I think it's positive that publishers review children's books in particular to make sure they reflect positive and respectful attitudes towards children.'
- Hazel Edwards' Australian classic is not the first children's book to come under scrutiny.
- 'The one I know about is the 'golliwog' being taken out of the Enid Blyton stories,' Mr Tucci said. 'Because it reflects racist attitudes and I think we understand as adults, books are a good way to learn.'

November 5th 2004

Hot topic on all morning TV programs. Western Australian media tended to ring two hours later because of the time zones. Often I did not see the interstate published articles or letters until much later, and I did not hear pre-recorded interstate or regional programs, nor how frequently they were repeated until anecdotal mentions later by people living in those areas.

But I was aware of Letters to the Editor in all newspapers. The issue had now reached poll status in The Sunday Age November 7th.

Age Online Poll

Children's Books: Should children's books be altered to reflect changing values?

Yes – 15%

No – 85%

Total Votes: 570

November 15th 2004

The 'Issues in the News' section of the weekly Education Age lift-out is a full page current issue discussion for secondary and upper primary students. The appearance of 'The Hippo Smack' on Monday November 15th was highly significant because this provided a range of views and the opportunity for students and educators to discuss the broader issues in a more balanced way. It also meant that most students were using the media clips as a clear thinking exercise.

Under the headline 'In a hippo trouble', it posed the topic 'The republication of a children's classic has raised questions about what young people should be allowed to read' with the questions 'Should children's books be censored?' and 'Is it fair to change Edwards' story?'

In its introductory paragraphs it noted that: Edwards' book is not the first to spark debate about the censorship of children's literature.

In July, Morris Gleitzman's children's books *Boy Overboard* and *Girl Underground* were criticised by Immigration Minister Amanda Vanstone. The books, aimed at nine to 12 year olds, deal with children in immigration detention centres. Ms Vanstone argued that the topic was not suitable for children.

There was concern that Gleitzman's books would turn children against the Howard Government's policy of the mandatory detention of asylum seekers and their children. But others argue that children already hear about the topic in the media, and books are a good way to engage young people on important social questions. They can help ease their anxiety about topics they don't completely understand.

The Australian Family Association disagreed. Its members said some issues, including abortion, war, abuse, bullying, divorce, homosexuality and alcoholism should be left to adults. It then quoted a range of views given in print and broadcast media:

> *'Talk about political correctness gone mad. One 'smack' hardly constitutes child abuse. If it works, don't fix it.'*
> Geraldine E. Foster, *Herald Sun*, November 6th

> *'Children should be allowed to be children. Their innocence should be protected.'*
> Bill Muehlenberg, Australian Family Association vice-president, *The Australian*, November 5th

> *'I don't think it's about censorship, I think it's acknowledging that decisions on discipline are up to parents and individual households.*

We didn't believe that keeping that line reflected the idea of choices that parents and guardians of children have to make.'
Laura Harris, Penguin spokeswoman, *The Age*, November 4th

'*Someone who crawls into their shell or suffers the pain of loneliness and rejection because their father 'growls at them' would not be a worthy heroine. As someone who experienced considerable violence as a child, I object to the issue being hidden away.'*
Ben Wheaton, *The Age*, November 4th

'*Smacking a child for drawing on a book is certainly an overreaction, but why can't we explain this to our children as we read it – 'Gosh, that's a bit harsh, isn't it?' and move on? This is what is wonderful about reading to our children; being able to talk over issues along the way.'*
Suzette Hosken, *The Age*, November 4th

'*Children see and hear things and they need ways to try and understand them. It is fantastic to have authors giving them tools with which to think about those things.'*
Agnes Nieuwenhuizen, *The Age*, September 6th

'*Young readers don't see political issues such as refugees and detention centres in the way that many adults do. Adults are often locked into the party political, left wing/right wing, I'm right/you're wrong, mindset. Young readers see these issues much more in terms of empathy and justice; what's fair and what's not fair.'*
Morris Gleitzman, children's author, www.morrisgleitzman.com August 20th.

The section concluded with the question for its student readers: 'What's your view? Do you think Hazel Edwards' book should be altered? Why? Is there a place for censorship in children's literature? Are there some topics that young readers should be shielded from? Submit your view online.'

Over the next few weeks, the affair generated plenty of discussion. The following are email extracts (with permission given to quote), phone calls, SMS and Letters to the Editor which are in the public domain.

Letters to the Editor (*The Age*)

Don't mess with hippopotamuses

While Hazel Edwards has been asked to make a seemingly minor change to her book, *There's a Hippopotamus on Our Roof Eating Cake*, (The Age, November 4th), she highlights a worrying trend in censorship of children's books.

'Daddy gave me a smack' in this context (a fanciful story) is unlikely to be taken to heart by a child, but if that child is in an abusive situation, he or she just might be able to name their problem because they have been given the language to express it.

Our society is reeling from the effects of older generations who are just now disclosing the sexual abuse suffered during childhood precisely because it was a problem that wasn't talked about in nice company.

A number of authors for older readers, such as John Marsden, have encountered censorship when their themes run to mental illness, suicide and other taboos. Their readers devour their books, hungry for subject matter that engages them.

We can't protect our children from everything, but let's at least allow them the tools to express themselves. Censorship is not the answer.
Linda O'Connor, Northcote

Sample email: Kathryn Duncan (Children's book reviewer, mother of two).

I thought you might be interested in a discussion I had with my daughter's kinder assistant after she saw the article in the *Herald Sun*.

Sam is of the opinion that you should leave it as smacking. She feels it is a good discussion point for children and can help them learn that smacking is in fact wrong (this is the way I have dealt with it with my daughter). Sam felt that a smack, in this context, does not constitute child abuse. We also talked about the fact that growling can be a form of mental/psychological abuse as well.

And a witty letter from The Age on November 8th 2004: PC Penguins

Well, everybody who is anybody knows that Daddy Hippos do certainly smack young Hippos that get onto the roof and eat cake. It is Mummy Hippos that growl in such situations. Any self-respecting

Penguin of whatever age should know that. Perhaps Penguins need to return the children's book publishing to Puffins, who would not tolerate such subtle censorship.

So, Hazel Edwards, don't let yourself be bullied by Politically Correct Penguins.

Robert Gunter, Red Hill

Emails were often addressed via my website and since it was not possible to gain permission to quote the writers in some cases, the points from these are summarised:

- ... I was dismayed to read that line 'Daddy smacked me' in your award winning book, and it has caused me to pass over the book in selecting stories to read to my children from our bookshelves at home ...
- Every time we read your book, the Daddy smacks the little girl – every time.
- The nature of children's books is that parents and children read and re-read them until they know them off by heart. And so, in this story, the message is that Daddy always smacks.
- An argument against changing the wording after 27 years is that many children know the words by heart. My son really loves any of the hippo stories of yours that we can find. He is nearly three and can say verbatim all the words in There's a *Hippopotamus on Our Roof Eating Cake*.
- You may have to remove the reference to eating cake to 'eating a low fat, no carbohydrate healthy snack alternative' for fear of encouraging childhood obesity.
- Let's promote education and choice, not prohibition and censorship.
- I draw a similar parallel to my situation as a composer, where I might be asked to change notes in my works five years hence, because somebody does not like a particular sound. I would most definitely not change my work; oh, how we could rewrite history!!
- Maybe they should change 'Daddy' to 'Father Figure' or 'Male Role Model' too. I mean, not every child has a Daddy, do they?
- ... while my daughter and I have enjoyed reading the original version of the book, that particular page did jar with me and influenced my decision not to buy that particular book to send to the daughter of a friend in the US knowing that they don't smack their own children or condone the practice. I just wanted to let you know that, while you are

probably hearing lots of criticism from the anti-PC brigade, there are other parents who support you and would probably be more likely to buy this book now. I am particularly pleased to see that such a lovely book will be available to a new generation of children.

Then it was drawn to my attention that there were other websites discussing the issue with a forum based on only an electronic extract:

June 1st 2005 a very colourful letter arrived:

Late last year I had the good fortune to meet Dr June Factor (former Civil Liberties Chair) at a social function. Your book which was attracting some controversy at the time came into our conversation. I told her about my nephew, as a three year old, and she suggested I tell you the story.

Martin sat down to 'read' *There's a Hippopotamus on Our Roof Eating Cake* as three year olds do who have heard a book so many times they know all the words and when to turn the pages. However, the Martin version was slightly different:

"There's a hippopotamus on Our Roof.' 'Shit!' said the mother."

As Martin's mother, my sister remarked, 'That's exactly what I would say!' Martin is 16 now, but the story lives on. Thank you for all the pleasure your books have brought my family over the years.

The ASA has discussed copyright issues with the Attorney-General who has accepted the view that Australia is bound by the Berne Convention on Human Rights to introduce Moral Rights, i.e. the right to be attributed as the author of a work, and the right to have the integrity of the work respected.

The latter provides authors with a legal right to object to the distortion or modification of a work which is prejudicial to the author's reputation.

This 'curious electronic eFair of the hippo smack' has raised issues of media escalation and interactivity of debate due to electronic availability, the impact of political correctness on children's books, censorship and most importantly, the imaginative power of a children's book which lasts into adulthood.

Case study: Young Adult novel f2m: the boy within

Controversial YA (Young Adult) Novel and Social Media Usage

f2m: the boy within required extra author involvement in marketing because of the controversial subject of gender transitioning. Social media such as Facebook, Twitter, blogs etc were an innovative match for the potential young adult audience.

Income earned, copies sold and film options are objective ways of evaluating the financial impact of a book. Even if more subjective, social media is an additional way in which controversial fiction with a small publisher may reach international readers, provoke reactions and subsequent sales.

Most fiction has a life of a year with maybe only a month of publisher driven media coverage. To survive, a book needs word of mouth recommendation, and to get that, readers need easy access to the book over a longer period. Social media provides a way of prolonging exposure, and indirectly adding sales.

Sequence of events

Ryan was a family friend whom I'd known since aged eleven and presenting as a girl. We kept in touch during his ftm (female to male) transition. When Ryan was 33, and happily married, we decided to co-write a novel – a novel not an autobiography. We chose Ford Street (www.fordstreetpublishing.com), a niche publisher of edgy YA fiction but with mainstream distribution, who offered an advance and contract from our one page proposal. We agreed to co-promote the book via social media and on the talk circuit. Across a year, two continents, and 40 drafts, *f2m: the boy within* was co-written via weekly plotting on video call and email. It was the first international YA novel on transitioning gender co-written by an ftm co-author.

The publisher sponsored a Melbourne library launch in February 2010 with both authors present for media opportunities and autographing. The second (July 2010) launch was in a New Zealand bookshop, strongly supported by the queer and transgender community, where I attended via video call and a local Member of Parliament was the launcher. Strong book sales and photo opportunities make a bookshop launch preferable to an electronic, virtual launch via blog tour.

The subject of transitioning gender was controversial but not the handling of the writing within this novel. So once the book was read, it tended to be recommended. The challenge was to get the book out there.

Things that didn't work include bookclubs not buying because of the subject, and the title being ignored by awards.

Our mistake was concentrating on the educational market. The gender counsellers, psychologists and specialised gender bookshops were a more significant channel. In New Zealand the book launch was supported by the queer and transgender community plus it was an online launch link between Australia and New Zealand, which was newsworthy.

We under-estimated librarians' fear of parental or religious criticism which meant the book was avoided, whereas my titles were usually ordered automatically.

Our self-funded speaking at an international librarians conference was a disaster due to formatting prescriptions, concurrent programming, no listing and badly organised bookshop supplies (not due to our publisher) but fortunately the visual presentation was later recycled.

Timing can be crucial: We had two professional development talks in late 'bad' time-slots when conference participants preferred to leave early to travel home or go for drinks. It is vital to get 11am slots for controversial/ thought provoking content, when participants are more receptive.

The expense of review copies and international postage needs to be taken into account. Our publisher was generous with copies but eventually we suggested eCopies with security, to save on postage.

However, some reviewers or judges couldn't cope technically with eCopies while some awards require airmailed reading copies for up to 10 judges, at international locations. This is costly, especially as some awards advertised as international are often found to be only USA orientated.

It is frustrating to have to deal with narrow mindedness such as the teacher who 'binned' 'this disgusting book' in front of secondary students. But, this led to:

- Candidly discussing this censorship in a high profile blog which gathered many positive comments.
- A Salon of Psychologists talk which led to (in progress) a documentary about reactions to the book.

Effective strategies for a controversial subject

What worked?

- Focusing on the 'process' of electronic collaboration and innovations rather than the controversial subject.
- Re-usable visuals in low and hi resolution of the cover and the co-authors.
- Re-usable show talk about social media with *f2m: the boy within* as the sample.
- An author website book pages with resources and links, updated daily
- Links to where the book could be bought in print and eBook formats
- Podcasts, tagged and cross referenced e.g. to ABC Life Matters.
- YouTube clip of the New Zealand book launch.
- eBook availability internationally.
- Utilising Ryan's IT skills in book trailer and using links.
- The speed of YA blogger-reviewers and guest blog interviews.
- Strategic reviews and recommended reading lists for gender issues such as the Safe School Coalition gender resources and Family Therapy awards.
- Curriculum links and teacher discussion notes.
- The launch cake with scanned book cover provided photo opportunities
- International three way web chats with rural youth and the co-authors written up online for a librarian site and linked.

Authorpreneurial Hint

Anecdultery: Keep a log of the fictional challenges, like choosing an apt title, creating a fake family history, genetic research, and plot your progress on a video call to use as anecdotes in later talks and articles.

Unexpected outcomes

Some unexpected outcomes inlcluded:

- 2011 White Ravens listing with mainstream top 250 YA novels internationally.
- Different genre panel invitation: AussieCon 4 invitation to be a panellist on transgender characters in a science fantasy context.
- Fan art character sketch by ftm graphic artist Sam Orchard.
- A USA Educators site requested teachers' discussion notes.
- Gender definition notes and activities created in response to: 'How could I share this book with adolescents when I'm not sure of the gender issues?' The suggestion was to create music to go with the punk song lyrics from the novel. Could this lead to a punk music lyrics contest/performance? Or could it be cast as a movie, an enactment of the school reunion bully scene? All these possibilities mean using literature as a way of opening up discussion one step removed from the individual kid with gender issues.

Our realisations

Winning a major award, preferably an international one, helps distribution. Review copies need to get to strategic listings, and that's an additional expense, and takes time for professional print journals to publish, by which time print copies may not be so freely available in shops. It is vital to have eCopies that provide long-term and easy buying online. In other words, an eBook definitely matters.

Advocates: If strategic people become advocates of your book, this is a significant boost, but it takes word of mouth time.

Co-authors in different countries have two networks and this means double value.

Reviews: These need to be linked immediately on each co-author and publisher website. A one liner extract plus a summary of all media to date in a print handout appeals to the print minded.

Emphasise the topical curriculum issue using the 'bullying' chapter as an introduction. Tackle prejudices head-on and use a suggestive title. For example, I wrote a mainstream article on 'What happens when you don't write what others expect' and was interviewed under 'The book libraries rejected.'

In our case, the collaboration was based on a similar work ethic, complementary skills and mutual respect.

Ryan's View:

'It was definitely a challenge to be co-writing a novel and working at a full-time job at the same time, but our skills and knowledge seemed to complement each other for a great working relationship. With my IT background I could easily put up a website to promote the book and how we came to write it, and set up Twitter, Facebook and web-monitoring tools (Google Alerts) to always know who was talking about us on the web and respond quickly, if appropriate. Once the initial PR is over, the work is only just beginning.'

5: Hypothetical Scenarios

These are some scenarios which might happen. What should you do if faced with a legal, ethical, timing or relationship dilemma? Should you seek advice, or take action?

➼ The Co-Coach Dilemma: Two sports mates have an idea for a small 'how to coach this sport' publication to accompany talks they are requested to give individually or together in their sports fitness industry. It includes common coaching tips but also the new approach to training beginners using diet and cross training, which they develop. Their families with young athletes are involved as case studies and in photographs and clips.

Demand grows, and they start selling 'Co-Coach' in varied formats. It becomes a full time business for one, but the other partner keeps their day job. They have a hand shake agreement to share costs 50/50. International and multi-media opportunities arise and there's conflict about who owns what. Each claim they contributed more to the concept, they genuinely can't remember who contributed which ideas, and the full timer wants the freedom to make all business decisions, especially as there has been a big financial offer for a film.

➼ TV Connections? While participating in an international literary festival, as an example of the creative process, the well published but slow writing author shares a concept for a multi-media mystery series, which he is currently researching. This is about a distinctive, psychologist/marriage celebrant sleuth, crossing into various cultures and has long-term potential.

Later, a multi-national publisher rejection arrives, despite the existing contract, due to another 'too similar' series, which has been translated and contracted for a television channel from a TV psychologist who attended the international festival, and was the MC on that literary panel.

- Two former teachers were romantic and business partners who developed a home based educational publishing organisation under their surname. Roles were specialised: he was marketing and she was the curriculum expert. They took out a big mortgage to build a well equipped office and storage extension to the house, but their marriage split meant that due to debts they had to continue working together in the same location.

- A parent writes, on behalf of their four year old, to the author, publisher and the newspaper to complain about the particular phrasing in a children's book, which they consider offensive. The parent asks the author to change the wording. The publisher speaks to the author, and considers withdrawing the book. Librarians move it off the shelves.

- A well known creator Z is especially bad at keeping records and files. A dispute arises with a former colleague X about ownership of intellectual property. Proof of the existence of Z's dated draft of that earlier manuscript is needed to check the inclusion of a character name. Z spends a week tidying workspace and can't find it. A year later the missing file is found, slipped down the back of a drawer, but it's too late, and the case is lost and X gains financially.

- An appealing child's photo is used on social media without permission as part of a book publicity, and goes viral.

- Fiction being considered autobiography is common. An ex in-law complains they have been portrayed as the 'wicked woman' in a novel, and the book is pulped. The author's next book is rejected because of potential 'legalling' costs.

- A student plagiarises a lesser known story by a well known author and wins the literary contest, and the monetary prize.

- The book of a 'celeb' for whom English is not a native language is 'ghosted' and wins a literary award for quality writing with significant prize money.

- A writer becomes involved in the community production of an adaptation of one of their published books. Actors improvise and translate, but the author writes the performance script and a later new book based on that concept. Later the local community theatre claims to own all rights in the work and wants to share royalties.

- A debut novelist with a topical issue is unable to interest a print publisher so publishes online, at their own expense, as an eBook. Sales are reasonable and subsequently a print publisher is interested, but not once it's known that the eRights have already been used.

- Books do not arrive in time for the launch due to a transport strike, Chinese New Year celebrations and a wrong address. Enlarging the cover, as a poster, holding a 'fake' book and taking orders are not enough.

- A writers' group meets regularly and critique each other's work and shares marketing tips etc. Although all are at a comparable level when they start the group, a couple begin to publish more widely than the others. Author A continues to share tips with the group and dominates with their chapters requiring editing, but Author B keeps marketing opportunities to herself. Then a more 'social' creator joins who wants to 'chat' rather than work. The group decides it's time to change the rules.

- An animation/film proposal requires considerable investment in latest technology samples, meetings and numerous drafts in order to attract overseas co-production, broadcasting and merchandising. The project is speculative, the producer has a good track record, strategic contacts and regularly attends rights fairs, but at what point should the writer put paid, small work ahead of constant speculative re-writes for a million dollar project which may never happen?

- The family complains that an author is work obsessed, and although they enjoy the book related research travel and income they are unsympathetic to the time required to write and market a project. Consequently adolescents may answer the business phone with grunts, forget messages or be rude to visitors. Partners may be fed up with publicity focusing on the author in the family. The writer's workspace is invaded by computer game playing children. Maintaining a better family/work balance requires changes.

- The extended family is embarrassed by published book revelations in a radio interview or TV news.

- An author is doing a radio talkback relating to a controversial issue in a recently published book. A caller, claiming to be a former lover, disputes the claims in the book and accuses the author of being hypocritical.

- Some of the subjects interviewed for a non-fiction book are unhappy about the presentation of their edited transcripts, specifically in the headings of their categories and wish to withdraw just as publication is close.

- An author/psychologist is accused of 'making up' case studies for a relationships book and of breaking client confidentiality in the detail of examples.

- A small, mainly online publisher has an incomprehensible royalties statement which does not itemise life sales of the title, and also includes charges for web hosting and eBook conversions and translations. Is this vanity publishing or bad accounting?

- Original artwork and memorabilia is requested for an exhibition held in a marquee within a festival, and is returned late and damaged. Who's responsible?

- Ego-Googling, an author discovers ePiracy of several of their out of print books, on a site in a different language and re-packaged within a series under an editor's name and asks the former publisher to chase up the legal situation. The publisher says it is not their problem as rights have reverted to the author.

- A writer has consistently requested reversion of rights on an earlier, now out of print series, as they have other titles prepared, and wish to re-publish in new formats. The earlier, small publisher has been taken over by a multi-national who was in turn 'merged' and no one answers about the status of their titles. Suddenly they discover via Googling that their titles are listed as 'orphaned' and available for anyone to use.

- An amateur portrait painter has copied the photograph of a local creator from the local newspaper, and entered their portrait for a community award and as part of a travelling exhibition. Suddenly their work's validity is queried. Do they have the permission of either the subject and/or the photographer, or the newspaper? Does the newspaper chain own the photographic rights or the contract photographer? Is the portrait required to be painted from life and do they need a release/permission form? They ring the Copyright Agency.

- A former dance champion with a considerable fan base, sets up a studio dance school specialising in Indigenous traditional dance which attracts government funding. Initially, she undercuts competitors, sharing the space with others who are not government funded. They refuse to deputise for her in emergencies or to refer other clients or to collaborate on costs for festivals which showcase their talents internationally.

6:
AUTHORPRENEURSHIP

A is for Author as creator of ideas

U is for Understanding or getting the facts

T is for an apt title

H is for a survival sense of Humour

O for Originality

R is for Research

P is for Professionalism

R is for Risk Taking

E is for Entrepreneurial

N is for Name as brand

E is for Energy

U is for Upskilling

R is for Recycling rejected concepts in new formats

S is for Small/Solo business of ideas

H is for Help-delegating

I is for Intellectual Property

P is for Profit

Miscellaneous Digital Tips from Peers

The fastest way to learn is from someone in a similar situation.

- Take note of responses via queries and workshops (not ones meant to promote brands, just strategies or techniques).
- Remember to get dressed before you answer any electronic appliance which has a camera.
- If co-ordinating video calls internationally for conferences or interviews, check on time zones, and local summer time changes. If the audio drops out, vote by signs, thumbs up for yes. Thumbs down for no.
- If you are adding more than two people to a conference call, charges may be involved but as long as one participant has paid, others may join. Alternatively, it may be possible to group speak via free audio but it helps to be able to see people's expressions.
- 'Ego-Googling'. Enter your name to check if your works are being pirated. It could be a compliment or a time consuming legal hassle.
- Self re-printing or re-publishing your backlists as eBooks is different from old style 'vanity' self-publishing. Authors taking charge of own backlist rights and re-issuing in digital formats is the future.
- In eBooks, name your chapters rather than number them and get a decent cover.
- A digital recorder is useful for own author talks, lectures and maybe podcasts.
- Ask for a demonstration with any eBook reader that claims to read PDFs regardless of what the instructions say. If it doesn't, it's useless for a travelling author.
- Do you need technical partners? You will need to decide on the upper limits of time or money you're prepared to spend or split work in kind. Alternatively, brand a series and pick technical and merchandising partners to share the risk.
- Learn the acronymns or ask if you don't know them. CMS (Content Management System) is just a template. DRM is Digital Rights Management (this is what you do with what you own). OCR is Optical Scan Recognition. It scans old books with no files although sometimes pirates do this too! App means a computer program application.
- Attend the free classes offered by various electronic suppliers and have questions prepared. Keep asking 'dumb' questions until you solve your specialised needs.

- Manufacturers frequently upgrade their devices which are then incompatible with yours. Decide what you really need and can afford for the job, and don't get into a status race with new toys. Decide if it is the process or the result which matters for you.
- Keep a running 'to do' list of technical challenges to solve when you have a free moment or are in the vicinity of expertise. Often interstate or city work allows 'an hour to kill' in between and can be used to solve a technical issue.
- There is an ethical issue around using international monopolies with easier and cheaper access versus 'Indie' locals who support your culture.
- Speed of change in formatting can be an issue and it is advisable to aim for material with generic usage that can be updated as technology changes.
- Non-exclusive electronic/digital rights to publishers is preferable as circumstances are changing fast and an author also needs to sell from their own site.
- Multiple language insertion is a viable possibility and if you have ethnic grandparents they can add their own language to eBooks which have literacy implications.
- A quality, niche market is needed for selected title development.
- iPads or similar are wonderful for fast, silent note taking during conferences. If a touch typer, you're seemingly giving the speaker most of your attention. Simple keyboard shortcuts include swipe upwards on the comma for single quote marks, or swipe upwards on the full-stop for double quote marks. If you are struggling to find other currency besides dollars on the numeric keyboard, simply hold down the $ symbol and alternatives will appear.

Procrastinating Toys or Tools of Trade for Electronic Junkies

Some opinions

Participating in an online forum style (written) adventure website honed my ability to develop a character. Members of the forum had to imagine a character and build that character's back story, abilities, personality and possessions in such a way as to interact with other characters on the forum in a realistic way. When the forum folded, I felt lost. (Lynda)

Video calls help me keep in touch with non-writing friends but more importantly with interstate and international colleagues. It saves travel time and cost. If asked for an interview, I suggest using video. I also do research interviews on video call. Sometimes I have to get up very early for London or USA calls. (June)

I never read the instructions. I just teach myself, working on my current project but using the new equipment. As a last resort, I ask a technician. Usually it takes me about 50% longer than the old way. (Charl)

After you've had your iPad a while, there are too many apps to scroll. The dock on your iPad can hold six apps. Just press and hold any app until they start to jiggle then drag your six favourite apps down to the dock and drop them there. (Bren)

Question: Is your favourite program just a procrastination tool? One writer asked me if Scrivener was just a procrastination tool when they heard about all these extra folders and images, but agreed they spent hours scrolling through the manuscript to locate scenes they wanted to change.

Another writer said the ability to switch Scrivener into full screen mode was brilliant because it covered the Facebook icon and they didn't have to see the flashing numbers come up when people responded to posts. For me, it's worth setting it up well because it becomes a powerful editing tool in a long work.

Answer: If the program works for you, use it but also include how long it takes to learn before you can return to original work.

One mother stated: The formula is a bit like children's birthday parties. The enjoyment should be greater than the amount of preparation, plus the mess to clean up.

$E > (P + M)$

Project = Idea + Electronics (not minus)

Early Procrastinators or Early Adopters?

Why waste time learning fancy quilling – your silly swirls won't replace oral story-telling.

We'll see.

Survival Code of Authorpreneurship

- Ensure you can spell and pronounce your occupation. Authorpreneurship is a big word and a growing concept.
- Self-employed? Then you can't complain about the boss's decisions. You are free to work any time, but do your sums about a rough hourly return for effort.
- Your work becomes your passion and vice versa. A primary producer in the growing of fresh ideas, 'authorpreneurship' is an acceptable way of saying 'gambling' with artistic friend benefits.

7: Therapy Writing: Map of Serendipity

The Map of Serendipity

When I put "serendipity" into my GPS it told me to wander towards Sri Lanka, but I was hoping for something more like a happy coincidence.

Serendipity is a happy coincidence and cartography is precise mapping with co-ordinates and a planned route. Juxtaposing a map and serendipity appears self-contradictory, but both can be mind mapping in the sense of an idea converging, even if the traveller is unsure at the start and meanders for a while before reaching the destination.

And often the passion is so great that others are affected and infected by the notion and adopt the imaginative model. Sometimes, but not always, it becomes commercially viable.

Sole/Soul Projects

'Soul' projects are often serendipitously significant. They are subjects about which the creator is passionate but they may not be commercially viable. Within 'authorpreneurship' where the emphasis has been upon commercially viable innovations, it's important to reserve space for the soul projects, which need to be written, by and for the creator.

However, financially and emotionally, most creators can afford only one project of this kind. Hence the play on the word sole/soul. This section provides rationales for very different projects.

One is the cathartic distraction of co-writing during terminal cancer. The second is a personal rationale for choosing creative work life that was delivered as a university graduation address, with the theme of 'mapping' a career.

Therapy Writing

Ask yourself why are you writing this? Therapy writing may be cheaper than a psychologist's hourly rate, and doesn't wear out friendships with repetition. Is it the process or the final work which matters more to you? Perhaps it is best to just start writing.

Cathartic writing is a kind of therapy for those who have suffered trauma. 'Writing it out' may be helpful in ordering experience, so the memories can be tolerated or managed, and the writer can move on. Even writing a eulogy or an obituary can be a cathartic or emotionally cleansing form of writing.

Passion driven, therapeutic writing often has one reader: the writer. Some may never go beyond your journal and moving from therapeutic to sharing, may never happen. If the writing is candid rather than egotistical, others may wish to read it as a vicarious experience in order to understand a particular mindset. But you can assume a small readership.

If the emotions are too raw, they will overwhelm any reader. Using humour doesn't make the subject less significant. Try a quirky or slightly distanced viewpoint. For example, create a conversation hour between a cat patient and the feline psychiatrist.

Writing from diaries kept during the experience provokes immediacy of the senses, but may need to be put into social, political or medical context. Ask yourself if there is a universal significance in this particular story.

Structure matters. Even the most tragic circumstances need a contrast of wit or a change of pace and an opportunity for the reader to absorb the implications, before another disturbing fact is added.

Forget stream of consciousness and edit and punctuate for clarity of thought and the reader's comfort as well as a mastery of that memory.

The difference between professional and amateur writing is that the amateur writes for themselves and their own enjoyment or release. The professional crafts their writing for a potential reader.

Creating fiction or 'faction' via satire, humour or mystery, is a method of utilising the depth and height of that 'real' experience.

If the 'life versus death' outcome is already known, or it is grief about loss, sharing the grieving needs to be presented as more than a 'what happened next' in chronological order. Decide what the basic conflict is that you are exploring and whether, for example, the theme is courage under extreme circumstances. Can you offer any hope at the end?

Cathartic Writing as Therapy: 'Formula for Murder'

The cathartic distraction of co-writing genre fiction during terminal cancer.

Co-writing is not unusual. But this mystery-writing project under the pseudonym of A. K. Aye was a cathartic distraction, during the terminal cancer of one of the four co-authors. Formula for Murder was self-published in memory of breast cancer patient, co-author and our friend Dr Maryse Rochecouste. Therapeutic writing can be cathartic, and of value for the process itself.

Maryse's cancer was diagnosed during our second year of co-writing and she wanted us to continue the project so we would have a subject to discuss that was not her health. The cruel irony was that we'd earlier given this condition to the central character Marta. We were going to scrap the whole project, but Maryse insisted we continue, and not even change the character's illness.

Having a genre structure like a murder mystery gave us a convention to use. Formula for Murder by A. K. Aye was launched by Sisters in Crime in 1995 and co-written by four women, two of whom were mother and daughter. Subsequently, copies were donated to various breast cancer charities with an explanation of how it was written.

The five year 'no arguments' process of co-writing and questions such as 'how did they fit around the screen?' seems to intrigue others.

Other questions posed include:

Why did we decide to co-write a murder mystery novel?

It started as the plot for a murder dinner party. On impulse, science post-graduate student Liz invited us to visit her bio-chemical lab because, 'it would be a great place to set a murder'. After visiting, we decided to plot a mystery set in the lab and perhaps use it as the basis of a game.

We spent weeks preparing dossier details for each of the major characters. Then we plotted the outline based on the deadly implications of a highly commercially significant drug formula being discovered in a university research lab. Our drug formula theme became very topical. Ironically we would sometimes create incidents for our plot and then find news items later which meant our 'fiction' was happening in 'fact'.

At first we used to meet for two to three hours on Friday nights at rotating workplaces. Once we started to work on screen, we tended to work in Maryse's study because she had the best computer.

It was fun and we laughed a lot. We regarded the project as a 'hobby' and we didn't really argue. Liz checked with her professor about using untraceable poisons and at one stage he was worried that she intended to use one rather than merely give it to our character. Barbara enjoyed researching details with Homicide and Maryse, who had published some academic works in French, found fiction a new challenge and a distraction from her illness.

Were the contributions equal?

In quality, but not necessarily in time. They were equal but different. As non-scientists, if we'd had to research the scientific background with which Liz was familiar, it would have taken months. She was able to instantly provide possible scientific clues like mistaking casein and KCN.

I was used to writing educational material and for children and my writing style is spare whereas Barbara and Maryse were fond of 'purple passages' of description. We keyed in the compromises and printed them out to take home and rework so we also recycled a lot of paper.

Four full author names on the cover would have been unwieldy.

And we had such long names. The name A. K. Aye was playing with words (a.k.a.) and ideas, it was short and unisex and it was also well up the alphabet. The setting of Melba University is fictitious and based on Dame Nellie Melba.

During re-writing, we constructed a timeline of events. This helped, but there were still inconsistencies so we decided on an enactment. Liz gained the university lab manager's permission for us to role play four deaths on two floors of the bio chemistry lab. We coerced 15 friends and relatives to play specific characters in selected scenes one Sunday afternoon. Each was asked to view the script from the viewpoint of 'their' character, act out the scene and discuss any inconsistencies. My daughter lay on top of the freezer (in a thick jumper) as she was the body of the character Amber.

Humorous hassles occurred. In our story, the crucial labs were all on the one floor whereas in real life, they were on several floors.

Our Animal Libbers protest scene in the car park was misinterpreted by university security who thought we were complaining about the real Animal House on the university property, especially as Maryse's husband was busy videoing the noisy 'protesters'.

The afternoon concluded with double helix shaped doughnuts and champagne in the lab tearooms.

Why did we decide to self-publish?

Because of Maryse's illness. We wanted her to be able to see a copy. Formula for Murder has been a 'best giver' (to various cancer charities) rather than a bestseller, but the process of therapy writing helped us, and others.

QUEST

This Monash University Graduation address to Arts Graduates (16 April 1998) shares the aspirational aspect of being a creator as a non-traditional work choice. It is also indicative of offering Arts Graduates insight into self-employment as a creator.

Chancellor, Vice Chancellor, distinguished guests, graduates, family and friends ...

'Quest' is the theme of my talk tonight. There's an African saying: 'Have patience, in time even an egg will walk.' To be in this hall today means that for many graduates, parents, family and friends, the 'egg' did indeed walk. The embryonic ideas, hopes and dreams which culminated in your presence here today, are the result of patience, persistence, talent and the development of skills. Yours and other peoples.

Dreams

Since you have graduated in the arts disciplines, you are potential idea-mongers: leaders and innovators in ideas worlds. There's a strong possibility that initiating self-employment may be a work style option for you in the next decade. And it's likely that you will need to be flexible enough to tackle new roles, some of which do not yet exist, nor do they even possess job descriptions.

Creators are our dream makers, those who suggest new perspectives which may apply to government, politics, management, health or the arts.

To influence reality, dreams must be structured and shared in a format others can understand. Creativity, technology and business are not in conflict, they are complementary.

A goal is a dream, with a deadline.

Today you've achieved one goal. But which route will you choose to your long-term aim? And how will you judge if you achieve your dream? Success?

So, what is success? And by whose standards?

Today is a public ritual which celebrates external achievement. On graduation day, a parent sighs with relief. And the graduate complains loudly about having to 'get dressed up' but secretly enjoys the fuss and acknowledgment.

But often a creator must judge success by internal criteria, the gap between the aspiration and the creation. What was the goal? Was it reached? How can it be done differently and more effectively the next time?

It has been said: an artist must know how far to go too far.

The journey you choose to take may follow a different route from others so it is unfair to judge 'success' or 'failure' by criteria to which the creator did not aspire.

Orienteering

I'm an occasional orienteer. Orienteering is the sport of running through the bush, using a compass and map to locate controls on a designated course. Route choice, navigation and speed are relevant skills. Elite orienteers are superb athletes, others aged five to 85, choose a course to suit their level of fitness, navigational skills and purpose.

Fast runners tend to choose the longer, but clearly defined flat paths. Good navigators 'bush bash' or 'red line', using a compass through the rough stuff and go directly to the control.

Naturalists meander, looking at the bird or plant life while show-offs run fast only at the finish, where crowds watch. Some are classified DNF (did not finish).

By some criteria, I'm a failed orienteer, because I get lost a lot, walk rather than run, make 180 degree compass errors, more than once, and I'm bottom of the W50 B category, which means that I'm probably the worst woman orienteer in Australia, aged 50-55.

My aims in orienteering differ from most others. I go at my own pace and admire the scenery. Try again if I navigate wrongly the first time. I exercise with my family and friends and as it's an individual sport I'm not letting down team members. Occasionally I collect story ideas and sometimes I jog-walk. But I rarely run in at the finish although I do eventually get all the controls. So orienteering works for me. It also gives me a hobby to list under author bio notes.

Decide on your route choice. Do you want to fast-track with a high profile and acknowledged results? Or do you prefer the 'rough' technical challenge of mentally finding your way around an idea? Risking an unorthodox route or way of travelling, as long as you have the eventual goal in sight, may be the way to go.

Why am I an author?

I like learning new things and having a legitimate excuse to be a participant-observer. I do not spend my life hunched over a computer. I have a laptop, mobile and an author website.

I've been hot air ballooning, gliding, flying in a Sikorsky helicopter to a Bass Strait off-shore oil platform, had an 'excursion' through a funeral parlour, visited a forensic lab, trekked in Nepal and learnt belly dancing ... all in the interests of research!

My initial choice of career was not made on financial grounds. I knew that writers didn't earn much but I wanted a varied work style that would be mentally stimulating and people centred.

I admit my major weakness is boredom with routine tasks ... especially formatting!

Although I won a scholarship, my family couldn't afford to send me to university. I left school at year 11 to work in a bank. My university degrees were studied part time while working, getting married and having a family. In between, I wrote and collected enough rejection slips to wallpaper the study.

The word QUEST is very appropriate for a writer:

Questioning Understanding Encouragement Serendipity

Traveller not just a tourist.

Q is for Questioning

Basically, I'm a sticky beak. I like to know about others' lives. Being a writer gives you a legitimate reason for asking questions. It then becomes respectable and is called research. After all, literature is just high gossip.

In turn, as an author of children's books, I'm frequently asked unusual and challenging questions. One of the most thought provoking questions I was ever asked came from an 11 year old.

'What would you do if you woke up one morning and your imagination had gone and your hands didn't work?'

I had to think for a while. Then I said, 'I would buy a digital recorder. Then I'd go on a quest in search of my imagination, because a writer can't create without an imagination.'

As an aqua-readaholic (I read in the bath), I'm on a seven books a week diet. I'd never contemplated living without the stimulus of other minds via the page or screen, until I was questioned by the mother of a five year old prep student in a remote country school. As an author, I'd been talking with the parents about 'encouraging your child to read.' About 30, neatly dressed, she waited until the others had finished, and then she asked nervously.

'Do you have any other books like *There's a Hippopotamus on Our Roof Eating Cake*? It's the only one I've ever read. Those words have patterns I can work out. My daughter is in Prep and learning to read ... I'm learning with her.'

What courage! Admitting illiteracy, especially near other parents who are readers. Luckily, there was a tactful librarian nearby and we found appropriate books.

That incident was a significant reminder to me. One idea can have the power to travel and influence others. But the skills to shape those words are also important and a courageous question must be answered.

The books I have written are not mine now. Once a book is published it has a life of its own and it may go places I have never been. I tend to think of it as a book-child, out on its own; an embryonic idea that has walked. It now belongs to the reader's imagination who re-creates from the thought clues designed in word-form by the author.

One of my greatest thrills has been to see my books in translation, or in another dimension such as in Auslan signing, or in a 'feelie' Braille picture book. And then to have the same stories performed by others with puppets, music and song. Ideas can travel.

Questioning is part of interview skills. Facts matter and so do answers, especially when you are the subject. But mistakes do occur.

In a country town which must remain nameless, I ran a workshop for historians on 'Writing a Non-Boring Family History' and explained that I was not a genealogist. The session was written up in the local paper as being conducted by gynaecologist Hazel Edwards. When I pointed out that I was not a doctor, the response came:

'Oh, it's only one end of life or the other!' Misconceptions can occur, if you don't check your facts.

Provocative questions also matter, especially if you address them to unusual minds. In the 'Gifted' program, the theme was 'Journeys' and I decided to reverse the common sequence of asking a question. Instead, I provided the answer.

'If the answer is a red journey, what is the question?'

A 10 year old said, 'My question is what happens when you start a purple journey but take away the blues?'

I enjoy working with unusual minds.

As a children's author I receive a lot of readers' requests.

'Dear Hazel Edwards ... we are doing a project on an Australian author. You were the last one left on the list. When were you born, did you get married and when did you die? I need this by last Wednesday ... no return address.'

It would have been difficult to answer that, posthumously.

U is for Understanding

Challenging stereotypes is an occupational hazard for a children's writer.

Psychologist Dr Helen McGrath with whom I wrote Friends, Love, Sex; A Practical Guide to Understanding Relationships which is about friendship, was asked recently 'Is it true that your co-writer is Hazel Edwards, the children's author?'

Helen said 'Yes.'

The response was: 'But the book's got 'sex' in the title. How can a children's author write about sex? Sex and children are incompatible!'

Stereotyping is limiting. It is preferable to think outside narrowly defined occupations or roles. Remember, 'web master', 'digital artist' and 'spin doctor' didn't exist ten years ago.

I write for adults, adolescents and children. It is harder to write well for children because each word counts. So does the design in conveying a complex idea, simply. You really have to know what you're talking about before choosing simple words to describe pyrotechnics, forensic science or even the way a hot air balloon works.

The skill to present complex ideas simply, requires a thorough understanding of the process. Whether writing fact, faction or fiction, it has to be logical. Even fantasy has an internal logic.

Ironically, children's writers are more likely to be economically viable, for they have a new readership every six years, earn more export dollars for Australia and have loyal followings. Children's authors receive more letters from readers, partly because adult fans tend to write to point out errors of fact. Child fans are honest, or touching.

> Dear Hippo,
>
> I haven't got a friend. Would you like to live on my roof? You could play sokker.
>
> Love Sam.

Children who have rich fantasy lives will become the adults who do not need stress management courses. They will also be the imaginative problem solvers in worlds other than books. They will design the bridges, aeronautical equipment and space food because they ask questions like 'What if?' and then attempt to provide a solution.

The logic of fantasy must be sustained within a book and between the reader and character. Often my characters receive mail. And it has to be answered.

'Corridor of Characters' was an Australia-wide touring exhibition of children's letters to my characters and the responses, in character. Letter writers gave permission, because letters belong to the writers not the recipient. Spelling was often idiosyncratic.

> Dear Stickybeak,
>
> Where were you before you were an egg? Love Joseph.
>
> That was a hard one to answer, for even a literate duck.
>
> Dear Joseph,
>
> Before I was an egg, I was an idea. Quack.
>
> From Stickybeak.

Artists and creators are not morally superior. Nor should they be seduced into believing they are instant philosophers. Their role is to provide a different perspective and allow individuals to reflect, and then act.

The issue of 'literary terrorism' faces all creators. This is the potential blackmailing threat that the artist will use her version of family affairs or romantic relationships, and call it 'fiction'. As if artists have a superior right to their version of intimate history which they don't.

An effective writer is androgynous, and can create credible characters of any age, occupation or gender, through the skills of research and observation plus imagination. The fiction writer who draws directly from real life, is limited, and will soon run out of material, friends, family and lovers. (But maybe more lawyers will be employed.) The novelist who is writing a novel about a novelist who is having trouble writing a novel indicates a limited lifestyle. A professional writer crafts 'composite' characters who have more intensity than any one person in real life, unless of course, the writer is a biographer or journalist.

E for Encouragement

Because creators often work solo, family support is important. I came from a family where books were valued, but I didn't meet an author until I was 23. I always knew I wanted to be a writer but I wasn't sure how. University wasn't economically possible for me and I had to leave school to go to work.

My father's legacy was the attitude that it was okay to be different, or to be the outsider, as long as you worked hard. Write only when you've lived a bit and have something to say. Ask questions and don't be intimidated by the labels on the doors.

As a teenager, I worked in our general store in Gippsland and learnt to talk to anyone and cope with whatever went wrong. What better apprenticeship for a writer. I pumped petrol, bagged pollard, weighed sugar, handled difficult customers and gave the correct change. These proved to be excellent survival skills for the business world.

Creators need partners who tolerate their idiosyncratic work styles. I've been lucky. They also need someone to understand the frustrations of rejection and rejoice in the successes. My husband and two children were very understanding about living with imaginary characters.

My publishers organised the making of a large hippo toy for promotional talks. Occasionally, between author tours, the large two metre high stuffed hippo travelled, seat belted in my car.

Unfortunately, one night we were waved down by the police breathaliser squad on Dandenong Rd. When they saw my front seat passenger, they said, 'Drive on Madame'. I'd only had a cappucinno anyway.

Currently I collaborate on different book, theatre and multi- media projects with three co-writers. We have equal but different skills. The ability to work as part of a creative team, contributing different disciplines is the future work style.

Computer linked, we alternate between meeting in person and via email attachments or video call. Collaboration overcomes procrastination and increases productivity. We also have fun.

S is for Serendipity

These are the happy events, that you didn't plan, but should stop and enjoy.

'S' is also for 'soul' projects the ones you do for pure enjoyment. Always program one into your schedule. Ironically they are often successful artistically and commercially because you invest so much energy in them.

T is for Traveller not tourist

Tourists just visit and expect to be entertained, travellers are participant-observers. Writers need to participate in life so they can write more realistically later. When things go wrong ... I tell myself this is research. As I trekked, upwards in the mountains of Nepal, I reminded myself, as the not so fit-trekker, 'This is research!'

Things do go wrong. Projects don't work out, despite business plans. The cheque isn't always 'in the mail'. Most writers learn to live with rejection. One proposal in ten is a good return. Some recycle the stories or projects and eventually they are completed while others give up, and become cynics or critics.

Success lies in achieving the goals to which you aspire. But your goals may not be the same as those of your neighbour in the seat alongside you today.

A creator needs to initiate work and be business-like not just 'be'.

Choose an unorthodox path as long as you know your eventual goal. In the long-term, satisfaction and pride in what you do is more important than external status.

Allow room in your life for 'serendipity', or fortuitous happenings. Recycle rejection, make something else happen and try again.

Make sure your equipment is in good order. On a quest, you'll need a backpack with essential supplies:

- Imagination: a creator should never leave home without it
- Torch: to illuminate good ideas
- Water bottle: to refresh with inspiration
- Strength bars for rejection times
- Compass or GPS to check on direction
- A memory bank card for recording significant experiences
- First aid kit: band-aid skills
- Luggage label ... so you know who you are ... and where you've come from or are heading.

Of course, the backpack needs to be versatile to act as armour, sleeping pillow, life raft, mobile advertisement and could even be edible. But preferably not see-through ...

Professional writing is not a career choice; it is a lifestyle decision to live more intensively, to be versatile, flexible and to work productively. To use your imagination in a way which might benefit others as well as yourself.

Today the egg walked. Tomorrow it may be part of some other creation. Poached, hard-boiled or rise in a soufflé ... hopefully with not too much hot air.

8: Additional Resources

The Australian Society of Authors website has a number of resources available for both members and non-members. Visit www.asauthors.org to access:

- Model publishing agreements templates.
- ASA papers on a range of writing and best practices topics.
- Information sheets on topics including royalty rates and conditions, agreements and contracts, the business of being an author and getting published.
- Links to Australian literary organisations, journals and magazines.
- Books and digital resources for authors.

About the Author

An avid reader (who read under the bedclothes as a young girl), Hazel Edwards wrote her first novel in grade six, a mystery about adventurous children stuck in a mine. After working in a secondary school and lecturing at Teachers' College, Hazel published her first novel aged twenty-seven, *General Store*.

It is Hazel's third published work that is her best known, the children's picture book classic, *There's a Hippopotamus on Our Roof Eating Cake*. This special imaginary friend has been cherished by children and parents alike and led to the dubious honour of Hazel being referred to as 'the Hippo Lady'.

Since its publication in 1980, the age-less Hippopotamus on the roof has been reprinted annually, evolved into a series of seven picture books, inspired a junior chapter book, classroom play scripts, a musical stage production and a short movie. The Hippopotamus books have also been translated into Mandarin, Braille, Auslan and were presented as an official Australian Government gift to the children of Princess Mary of Denmark.

Whilst Hazel loves creating quirky, feisty characters for newly independent readers in her easy-to-read junior chapter books (such as *Sleuth Astrid: The mind-reading chook*), she writes for all ages and has published over 220 books across a range of subjects and genres.

Hazel has collaborated with experts to publish adult non-fiction titles such as such as Difficult Personalities (now translated into seven languages), helps people craft memoirs and family histories by *Writing a Non-Boring Family History* and co-wrote *f2m:the boy within*.

Awarded the Australian Antarctic Division Arts Fellowship in 2001, Hazel travelled to Casey Station on the Polar Bird. This visit inspired a range of creative projects including the young adult eco-mystery *Antarctica's Frozen Chosen*, picture book *Antarctic Dad* and the memoir *Antarctic Writer on Ice*.

A fan of interesting and unusual locations, Hazel has been a guest writer-in-residence at the former Fremantle Prison (now the Fremantle Children's Literature Centre), the Mount Newman mining community in outback WA, a visiting author to Pasir Ridge International School in Indonesia and an author ambassador to Youfu West Street International School in Nanjing, China.

Passionate about literacy and creativity, Hazel has proudly held the title of Reading Ambassador for various organisations. Formerly a director on the Committee of Management of the Australian Society of Authors, Hazel was awarded an OAM for Literature (2013) and Monash University awarded her the Distinguished Alumni for Education (2022). Currently she is patron of the Society of Women Writers (Vic).

Hazel writes a new story for her four grandsons each birthday.

In 2024, Hazel is celebrating a Golden Anniversary, 50 years since her first book published.

Milton Keynes UK
Ingram Content Group UK Ltd.
UKHW020906220424
441551UK00009B/881